D0512047

Richard Harries was Bishop of Oxford from 1987 to 2006. On his retirement, he was made a Life Peer (Lord Harries of Pentregarth). Currently the Gresham Professor of Divinity and an Honorary Professor of Theology at King's College London, he is also an Honorary Fellow of the Academy of Medical Sciences and the Institute of Biology. He was a member of the Nuffield Council on Bioethics and the Human Fertilisation and Embryology Authority (HFEA), for which he chaired the Ethics and Law Advisory Group. SPCK has published a number of his books, including *God Outside the Box* (2002) and *The Re-enchantment of Morality* (2008).

QUESTIONS OF LIFE AND DEATH

Christian faith and medical
intervention

RICHARD HARRIES

First published in Great Britain in 2010

Society for Promoting Christian Knowledge
36 Causton Street
London SW1P 4ST
www.spckpublishing.co.uk

Copyright © Richard Harries 2010

All rights reserved. No part of this book may be reproduced or transmitted in any
form or by any means, electronic or mechanical, including photocopying, recording,
or by any information storage and retrieval system, without permission in
writing from the publisher.

SPCK does not necessarily endorse the individual views contained in its publications.

The author and publisher have made every effort to ensure that the external website
and email addresses included in this book are correct and up to date at the time
of going to press. The author and publisher are not responsible for the content,
quality or continuing accessibility of the sites.

Scripture taken from the NEW AMERICAN STANDARD BIBLE® (NASB),
copyright © 1960, 1962, 1963, 1968, 1971, 1972, 1973, 1975, 1977, 1995 by
The Lockman Foundation. Used by permission.
Extracts from the New English Bible (NEB), copyright © The Delegates of the Oxford
University Press and The Syndics of Cambridge University Press, 1961, 1970.
Used by permission.
Extracts marked NJB are taken from The New Jerusalem Bible, published and
copyright © 1985 by Darton, Longman & Todd Ltd and Doubleday & Co.,
Inc., a division of Random House, Inc. and used by permission.
Extracts from the Revised English Bible (REB), copyright © Oxford University Press and
Cambridge University Press 1989.

Every effort has been made to seek permission to use copyright material reproduced in
this book. The publisher apologizes for those cases where permission might not have
been sought and, if notified, will formally seek permission at the earliest opportunity.

British Library Cataloguing-in-Publication Data
A catalogue record for this book is available from the British Library

ISBN 978–0–281–06241–6

1 3 5 7 9 10 8 6 4 2

Typeset by Graphicraft Ltd, Hong Kong
Printed in Great Britain by MPG

Produced on paper from sustainable forests

*For former colleagues
on the Human Fertilisation and Embryology Authority,
especially Emily Jackson, Neva Haites,
Maybeth Jamieson and Shah Nebhranjani*

Contents

Preface

Some 250 years ago the French philosopher and art critic Denis
Diderot (1713–84) foresaw the existence of a warm room
whose floor was covered with little pots, and on each of these
pots a label: soldiers, magistrates, philosophers, poets, potted
courtesans, potted kings.

In 1968 I reviewed a book by G. Rattray Taylor, published in
that year, which predicted that Diderot's vision would come true
by the year 2000. This has not in fact happened. Nevertheless the
pace of scientific advance in recent years has been phenomenal,
and to many people deeply disturbing. In 1990 the Human
Fertilisation and Embryology Act – designed to regulate all
activity in this area that involved the creation of embryos outside
the womb – came into existence. It proved itself a remarkably
robust piece of legislation; nevertheless scientific advances
since 1990, together with various social changes that have
taken place since then, made it necessary to bring about a new
act, which came into force in October 2009. I had the privilege
of serving as a member of the Human Fertilisation and
Embryology Authority from 2003 to 2009 when some of these
momentous changes were discussed and regulated. The first
chapter of this book is deeply indebted to that experience.

The second chapter, on abortion, deals with an issue that has
obviously been around for much longer, and one about which
the Church has taught since the first centuries of the Christian
era. Not only did the Church have to give teaching in general,
it had to offer guidance to confessors about what penalties
priests should enforce if a woman confessed to having had
an abortion. These penalties are revealing, for they indicate a
much more nuanced attitude to abortion than is often assumed
to be the case. This has a bearing on how we regard the moral

status of the early embryo both for assisted reproduction and abortion itself.

The question of suicide has also been around a long time. The Stoics in ancient Rome thought that in certain circumstances the taking of one's own life was the right and honourable thing to do. However, over the last 50 years the pressure has grown to allow people who are dying, and who find life intolerable, to take steps to end their own life, rather than waiting for nature to take its course. This pressure has only intensified in the last ten years, and there have been two attempts in the House of Lords to bring in legislation to allow it. The third chapter of this book is clearly indebted to my having had the opportunity to be involved in those debates, some of which have been of a very high standard. This is clearly an issue that is not going to go away.

This is a book written from a Christian and, more particularly, an Anglican ethical perspective. In it I look at the scientific advances in the field of reproductive technology and research which can strike us as so disturbing, as well as at the other changes which have taken place. For a view of the wider ethical context in which these debates take place today, and the medical law since all the recent legislation, the definitive book on the subject is by Emily Jackson,[1] to whom I am grateful for having read the text and for her suggestions. I am also grateful to David Archard for reading the text and for his comments.

1
THE BEGINNING
OF LIFE

The cry of Hannah

Hannah was childless. Time and again she and her husband had tried for a child but failed to conceive. Hannah felt her childlessness to be a great shame and reproach, and other women taunted her to the extent that she wept continually and could not eat. Her husband was a kindly man and said, 'Am I not more to you than ten sons?' But she would not be consoled. One day she poured out her heart to God in such distress that the priest thought she was drunk.

Hannah, whose story is told in the first chapter of the book of Samuel, is just one example of women in the Bible who were in extreme distress because they could not have children. Sarah, Abraham's wife, was one; Elizabeth, the wife of Zechariah, and eventually the mother of John the Baptist, was another.

In some respects the situation today is different from that in Sarah and Hannah's time. Now a couple can decide not to have children without this being perceived as a stigma. If they try for children and fail, they will not be taunted. In biblical times, in Israel, continuing the family line through children was regarded as of paramount importance. Besides, with no health service or welfare state, you looked to those children who survived the very high early mortality rate to take care of you in your old age. But all that having been said, there are many couples today who are desperate to have children and who find it very difficult or impossible to conceive. This is a source of great sadness to them.

The chances of conceiving diminish with age, and in our society people are getting married much later. They may have a number of relationships before they find the person with whom they want to share the rest of their life. During that time, according to our current mores, they can live together and have a full sexual life without this entailing children. When they do eventually find the right person with whom to settle down the couple may perhaps wait for several years before having children. The wife has a career which she wishes to pursue and the couple may have a mortgage which takes two incomes to service. So people are not trying for children till much later. In 1990 just 3 per cent of first-time mothers were over 35. By 2002 the figure had risen to 10 per cent. This means that there are a good number of people in their middle to late thirties who feel they are ready to have children, but find that children don't come. It is no good being moralistic about this and saying they ought to have thought about it long before and had children in their twenties. We need to think seriously about the implications of postponing childbearing, but few would want to go back to a world in which a woman's only option was to be a wife and mother.

That the chances of conceiving diminish with age is due to a number of factors, such as the probability that sex will take place less often and the woman will produce fewer eggs, but there are other features of our society that have a bearing on couples' ability to conceive and which give rise to concern. The rising incidence of obesity and the increase in sexually transmitted diseases lead some experts to predict that infertility is on the increase and may even double in the next decades.

Whatever the causes, the result is that more people than ever are looking for medical help to produce children. Assisted reproduction is on the increase.

Louise Brown is a 31-year-old postal worker in Bristol. You may recognize the name. Born in July 1978, she was the first baby produced as a result of in vitro fertilization (IVF) through the pioneering work of Patrick Steptoe and Robert Edwards. The technique, in its broadest terms, involves stimulating a woman to produce a number of eggs, extracting these from her body and fertilizing them in a glass container, that is, *in vitro* as opposed to *in vivo*, in a live body. The fertilized egg may then be allowed to develop a little before being implanted in the womb. It sounds easy but it isn't. The process of stimulation carries slight risks. Very occasionally a woman is hyperstimulated, which can be dangerous. The process of extracting eggs and implanting the embryo in the womb is invasive and not totally comfortable. It is also expensive, averaging £3,000 per cycle of treatment. Nevertheless it has succeeded in bringing thousands of women what they so desire – the gift of a baby.

There are a number of other forms of treatment offered by fertility clinics which need not be considered in detail, such as ICSI – intracytoplasmic sperm injection, and GIFT – gamete intra-fallopian transfer. But the best known and most often used is the one I have described, IVF. This can be used as a model for the ethical dilemmas raised by nearly all forms of fertility treatment.

Robert Winston's book *A Child Against All Odds*[1] reminds us of what it is very easy to forget, that the pioneering work of Steptoe and Edwards met a great deal of disapproval from a conservative medical establishment as well as a fair amount of opposition from the general public and in Parliament. So let me first of all analyse a feeling that was around a great deal then and is still present to some extent today, that all this is unnatural; that it is playing God. We should simply leave something as fundamental as the creation of life to God-given nature. This is an argument which emerges even more emotively in subsequent scientific developments related to IVF, such as research on embryos to produce stem cells and preimplantation genetic diagnosis (PGD) to choose healthy embryos. These techniques are described later, together with the separate ethical issues they raise. But they raise in an even sharper form the question of whether what is done is in some sense 'unnatural'.

While it is understandable that people might feel these techniques are unnatural, it is a feeling that cannot stand up to rational analysis. First of all: what is nature? If you look at almost any landscape in the world, what you see is not simply nature left to its own devices. Most landscapes are the result of the interaction of human beings and the natural world over thousands of years. If you consider all our most familiar species of animals or crops, they have not come about simply by letting things be. They have emerged by careful breeding over many generations. Furthermore, when it comes to our own human nature, absolutely basic to it are our God-given brains. Our nature is to use all our skills to interact with the processes of the natural world in order to enhance human life. This is of course the basis of all medicine and has good precedent. In the book of Ecclesiasticus, the medical scientist is praised for taking compounds from the earth and using his skill to utilize them for healing:

> Value the services of a doctor for he has his place assigned him by the Lord . . . his skill comes from the Most High . . . The Lord has created remedies from the earth, and a sensible man will not disparage them . . . The Lord has imparted knowledge to mortals, that by their use of his marvels he may win praise; by means of them the doctor relieves pain and from them the pharmacist compounds his mixture. There is no limit to the works of the Lord, who spreads health over the whole world.
> (Ecclesiasticus 38.1–8, REB)

For us human beings with our God-given brains and skill it is not natural simply to let nature take its course. What is natural is using what we have been given to interact with natural processes for the good of humanity – and, we must add today, for the good of the planet.

However, there is still some feeling around that while this may be true as a general principle applicable to most of what we do, matters of life (and, as we shall see later in this book, death) are God's territory, and to trespass on them is an act of hubris which we perform at our peril. Now it is quite true that the creation of new life, especially human life, is awesome and miraculous, as well as mysterious, but this does not preclude us from using our God-given minds to find out the processes at work and perhaps help them achieve what they are designed to do. The unconscious mistake still made by many, alas, is that the more human input there is, the less there is of God, and that these are mutually exclusive factors. But in words first said by Charles Kingsley and later taken up by Austin Farrer, God doesn't just make the world, he makes the world make itself. In us that process of making becomes conscious. God works through secondary causes – in this case through our brains as they are deployed in scientific medicine. We are called to use our skills, not as an act of hubris, but as a gift in cooperation with God, for human well-being: and that includes the sphere of human reproduction.[2]

The moral status of the early embryo

In vitro fertilization raises a number of concerns, but above all it causes us to think about the moral status of the early embryo. Because of the public disquiet over the new techniques associated with IVF and the new possibilities that it opened up, the government set up the Warnock Committee, chaired by Mary, now Baroness, Warnock, which reported in 1984. The committee's main recommendations passed into law in the 1990 Human Fertilisation and Embryology Act, which governed all treatment and research involving the use of embryos outside the body. Since then there have been a number of dramatic scientific advances with profound social implications. Nevertheless the 1990 Act proved itself to be a remarkably robust piece of legislation and has provided a sound framework for regulating both treatment and research. It not only set up a regulatory regime for treatment but allowed research on early embryos, under licence, if such research could be shown to be necessary or desirable for improving fertility or reproduction. Later, through hotly debated regulations discussed in Parliament in 2001–02, the purposes for which research on embryos could be undertaken were expanded to include serious diseases. This research aspect of the bill understandably aroused particular disquiet and gave rise to a widespread unease about where it would all end. Here we come up against an example of the slippery-slope argument. 'Yes, this may be justified,' it is said, 'but it will inevitably slide into other forms of research or other ways of treating the early embryo, which are not acceptable.' I take this argument seriously, and will consider it both later in this chapter and in the chapter on end-of-life issues.

The 1990 Act not only provided a legal framework, it also set up the Human Fertilisation and Embryology Authority

(HFEA), with responsibility for regulating the whole fertility sector. This entails licensing all clinics, now numbering 136, and undertaking regular inspections. The HFEA is also responsible for data collection, and for ensuring that every research project involving early embryos is carefully scrutinized to ensure that it meets the requirements of the Act.

After extensive consultation over many years by the Department of Health and the HFEA and after long and serious discussion in Parliament, a new Act was passed in 2008, which came into force, together with a new Code of Practice from the HFEA, on 1 October 2009.[3]

Treatment, as I have already said, involves collecting eggs from the woman and fertilizing them with a view to implanting at least one of them in the woman's fallopian tube. It may be that eight or so eggs will have been fertilized, of which perhaps four show signs of chromosomal abnormality and will not be suitable for implantation, and two will be kept and frozen for future use. This may be done because the first attempt to become pregnant does not succeed and so the two frozen embryos can be used for another attempt, avoiding the necessity of going through another cycle of stimulation and egg collection; or it may be that at some point after a first successful pregnancy, the couple might decide they would like more children and again it will be possible to implant a previously frozen embryo. If at the end of the statutory period of storage – currently ten years – the eggs have not been used, and an extension has not been requested because of special circumstances, those eggs will be destroyed. So any process of assisted reproduction involving IVF will result in the destruction of some embryos, those that are not suitable for implantation and those which are suitable but which after a period of time have been shown not to be needed by the couple, not donated to others, or not given for research. This raises a fundamental ethical question about the moral status of the early embryo. Is this a human person who is being destroyed? Is this murder?

When the sperm comes together with the egg and fertilizes it, that tiny entity, smaller than a pin head, starts to divide and multiply. After about 14 days a tiny streak (the 'primitive streak') can be seen at one end of this bundle of cells, and this is the beginning of the nervous system. Up to 14 days these dividing, multiplying cells also go to form the placenta and umbilical cord, and can result in one embryo or in identical twins.

Fourteen days, or the formation of the primitive streak, whichever is earlier, is of crucial legal importance, and also, I shall suggest, of moral significance in itself. This entity from 0 to 14 days old I shall call the early embryo. Other names have sometimes been suggested, such as pre-embryo, but this seems to be the most neutral description. It is important to have a description that is as neutral as possible because language often has built-in assumptions which assume a conclusion that is open to dispute. For example, suppose the entity was called 'a person'; this would imply to most people that it had all the rights of an adult. If, on the other hand, it was simply termed 'a bundle of cells', this would imply that it could be treated like any other cell, and had no special status. So what we are considering in this section is the moral status of the early embryo. For the period after 14 days in the womb, I shall use the word foetus.

The Roman Catholic view, as expressed in the Catholic Catechism, is that 'Human life must be respected and protected absolutely from the moment of conception.' In other words, the right of the fertilized egg to life is the same as that of a foetus in the womb, a baby or an adult. This view is shared by many conservative evangelicals and some respected theologians of a variety of Christian traditions. It is a view vigorously expressed through various pro-life organizations, as they term themselves.

What we think of today as the Roman Catholic view, however, only took that form as late as 1869 under Pope Pius IX.

Before that, in the Christian West, the attitude to the early embryo was much more nuanced. Of course, Christians in earlier periods were not in a position to consider IVF, but they did have the issue of abortion to make judgements about. Abortion was always regarded as a sin, but in the West, for most of Christian history, a distinction as to the moral seriousness of abortion was drawn depending on whether it was early or late. There were two underlying reasons for this. One was the theory of delayed ensoulment. According to Aristotle, in a view taken up by Thomas Aquinas, we are first of all a vegetable soul, then an animal soul; only after 40 days (in the case of a man) or 80 or 90 days (in the case of a woman) do we become a human soul. On this view, then, the loss of the early embryo would not be regarded as the loss of an ensouled being, a human person.

The other reason was the old Latin translation of Exodus 21.22. This verse concerns a woman who loses her foetus as a result of a scuffle. It says that if the foetus is unformed, the penalty for the person responsible is financial, but if the foetus is developed, it is counted as murder, and therefore the penalty is death. This is not in fact what the Hebrew text means and is not what is conveyed by the later Latin version, the Vulgate, or modern translations, but it was influential during the formative period of the Church's thinking. So, for example, St Augustine wrote:

> If what is brought forth is unformed (*informe*) but at this state some sort of living, shapeless thing (*informiter*), then the law of homicide would not apply, for it could not be said that there was a living soul in that body, for it lacks all sense, if it be such as not yet formed (*nondum formata*) and therefore not yet endowed with its senses.[4]

Today we no longer believe in Aristotle's view of delayed ensoulment, nor do we use the old Latin translation of Exodus 21.22. But the fact that the Church in the West for most of its history

11

took a gradualist approach to the moral status of the embryo and made a distinction between the early and the developed stage, remains significant. Also, while earlier Christians were dealing with abortion and therefore with degrees of wrong-doing, IVF and modern research using early embryos is weighing the potential destruction of some embryos against great benefits, actual and potential. So while the Roman Catholic view needs to be taken seriously and carefully considered, I do not think therefore that we can take it as the definitive view of the Christian Church.[5] It is true that abortion has always been regarded as a sin. But in making a distinction in its moral seriousness, with the death penalty for a late abortion and a financial one for an early abortion, the Church was not thinking of mitigating factors in the behaviour of the mother. The difference in moral seriousness was due to the difference in moral status of the embryo, depending on whether it was developed or undeveloped.

Although we do not share the philosophical background or biblical interpretation that was used to justify this distinction, the point is that mainstream thinking in the Western Church, from at least the fourth century – and in my view earlier – until 1869, took a gradualist view towards the moral status of the embryo.[6] In other words the Church took the view that the status of the embryo was linked to its state of development. This poses the obvious question about when that embryo gains the status of a human person. The law in England says that it is at birth, with babies now being viable from 24 weeks, and babies born at 23 or even 22 weeks occasionally surviving. Roman Catholic teaching says personhood is acquired at fertilization. But many people are not happy to take either of these pole points for the emergence of personhood. They think that it is at some point in between that we should regard what is in the womb not just as a foetus but as an unborn child, even though they find it difficult to say at just what point this is.

There are also wider arguments that bear on the question of the moral status of the early embryo. First, it has been discovered that as many as two-thirds of fertilized eggs may be lost naturally. This is nature's way of doing its best to ensure that only healthy embryos get implanted and come to term. So when an IVF practitioner looks through a microscope at the fertilized eggs and, for example, selects two for implantation, discarding half a dozen that appear to have some kind of damage, he is doing in a more scientific way what nature does anyway.

For me the high rate of loss of fertilized eggs in nature raises theological questions. If each egg is to be regarded as a human person – that is, an eternal soul – it leads to the extraordinary situation in which heaven is mainly populated by people who have never been born. On the other hand, if the God-given nature that has produced us is prodigal, it makes sense to work with that prodigality to refine natural processes, in order to bring into being healthy babies rather than damaged ones.

This argument is, I think, further reinforced by the mourning customs of most societies. We know for certain that the birth of a stillborn baby brings great grief. We also know that the loss of a baby, even when an abortion has been chosen, can be deeply traumatic. And we know that even a very early miscarriage can bring great sadness, particularly for a couple who are longing to have a child. Nevertheless, with the possible exception of Japan, no society in the world has formal burials and mourning rituals for early miscarriages. This is not a decisive argument against treating such losses as the loss of a human person, but our instincts about such matters may help to give us common-sense wisdom in this area.

A second argument has to do with what happens at the formation of the primitive streak. Before that time, as already stated, some of the cells go to form the placenta and umbilical cord and may divide into more than one embryo. After 14 days, with the early embryo implanted in the womb, we can say that we have a human individual. We can look at a photo of ourselves as a child and say, 'That was me when I was one.' We can look at a photo of the foetus in the womb and say, 'That will be our child.' But before 14 days, it is not possible to make a statement like that about the tiny bundle of dividing, multiplying cells. It is only after 14 days that we have a distinct individual.

A third argument has to do with the relation between what is potential and what is actual. A student at university is a potential graduate. But she does not have the rights of a graduate until she has passed her exams and obtained a degree. A 14-year-old is a potential voter, but he is not entitled to vote until he has reached the age of 18. The early embryo is human life with the potential to become, after the formation of the primitive streak, a human individual. The question of whether that human individual has the full rights of a human person or whether those rights only accrue when the baby comes out of the womb (or even later) will be considered further in the chapter on abortion. For now the point is that the early embryo, that is, up to about 14 days, is not yet an identifiable human individual and has no rights.

This does not mean that the early embryo should be treated as so much human waste. The Warnock report recommended that the early embryo should be treated with respect, and this is the basic assumption behind having an Act which regulates all fertility treatment.[7] It does not mean that the embryo should never be destroyed. What it means in practice is that every embryo has to be treated responsibly and accounted for. If the embryo is to be destroyed at some point, a reason has to be given, and disposal has to be carried out with 'appropriate sensitivity'.[8]

The position I take here, which is indeed the position taken by the mainstream reports of the Church of England, is often labelled a gradualist one.[9] This indicates that an increasing degree of respect, and therefore of protection, is due to the embryo as its potential is realized. There is nothing unique about this. When we walk by an oak tree we think nothing of treading hundreds of acorns into the ground. But someone who destroys a fully grown oak tree without good reason is rightly regarded as a vandal. Indeed we sometimes place preservation orders on grown trees in a way that we would not for a sapling, unless it was of a very rare species. In fact, the idea of basing a view of the foetus solely on its fertilization or birth when there is such extraordinary change and development between these two points is odd. As Peter Byrne has written, 'It is surely implausible to suppose that the whole moral question rests on what happens to one or other of the extreme points between which massive biological development occurs.'[10]

A possible person?

While the official Roman Catholic opposition to all forms of IVF is clear enough, a more subtle justification of this opposition is put forward by some Roman Catholic theologians, and a few others. This focuses on the uncertainty of the status of the early embryo, and the fact that it might have the status of a person. Because of this uncertainty, so it is argued, we should act with all possible caution and treat the early embryo as though it was in fact a person. Robert Song, for example, who would I think define himself as an Anglican evangelical, uses the analogy of a factory which is to be demolished and in which, it is learnt, children might be playing. He argues that it would be immoral to demolish the factory until we are absolutely certain that there are no children there.[11]

One possible argument against this is that if the need to demolish a building was of great necessity, say in wartime, then it would not be an overwhelming priority to ascertain first that there were no children in the vicinity. The analogy with IVF and using embryos for research is that there is a good, pressing reason for doing this. It is not a trivial reason.

15

Mary Warnock takes a different approach. She writes that Song, like others who argue from the issue of uncertainty or on the balance of probabilities in the dispute, is confused, because the word 'person' is already, as John Locke put it, a 'forensic term'. Its use entails that rights have been accorded to it:

> Yet it is often used as though to say of someone (or some corporate entity) that it is a person is to state a matter of observable fact, not a matter of law. It is as if we have come upon a body in a sack and are not sure whether it is a human body or that of some other animal. If we are contemplating throwing it out to sea we ought to make sure first whether or not it is a human, for to be willing to throw away something that for all you know is a human being is to be willing to risk throwing away a human being. And in such a case we certainly should open the sack and uncover the body so that if necessary we can give it a decent burial. But we cannot in the same way simply discover whether the embryo is a person.[12]

My own view is that at any rate from fertilization to 14 days it is not appropriate to use the word person, and for the reasons adduced above it is not appropriate either to talk of a possible person. Another approach which reaches this conclusion is that of Anthony Kenny, when he discusses the more sophisticated position of some Roman Catholic theologians such as Norman Ford and the response to them of David Jones. Ford is opposed to research on embryos; nevertheless he has argued that individual life cannot begin at a stage when an embryo may well split into a pair of twins. Jones's response to this is that an embryo is an individual living being which has a certain power – that of twinning – which is lost in later life. Kenny comments:

> But to count embryos is not the same as to count human beings, and in the case of twinning there will be two

different human individuals each of whom will be able to trace their life story back to the same embryo, but neither of whom will be the same individual as that embryo.[13]

Persons, souls and God's call

Many people, not just Christians, believe that we have souls, and the Christian Church has long taught that we are both body and soul. Some people have believed that the soul pre-exists our birth, for example Plato and admirers of his such as the early Christian theologian Origen. This view appears in the Book of Wisdom where Solomon says, 'I was a boy of happy disposition, I had received a good soul as my lot, or rather, being good, I had entered an undefiled body' (8.19–20, NJB). But in recent decades any talk about the soul has come under increasing scrutiny, on the one hand from philosophers and on the other from those who study the brain. It seems difficult either to make much sense of the word soul or to identify where such a thing might reside. The philosopher Gilbert Ryle seems to have demolished once and for all the idea that the soul is a kind of box inside a box inside us. Nevertheless, 'soul language' is still important in preserving an essential feature of what it is to be a human being, even if our starting point must be very different from that of most people in the past. Our starting point is the modern emphasis on the integral relationship between the brain and the mind, and the fact that we are through and through material beings. This obviously raises a major question about our capacity to think and choose, and to direct our lives in any real sense. But without denying the physical basis of our mental functions there is today also an emphasis on the possibility of what has been called 'top-down causation'.

Most emphatically this view does not deny the material, physical basis of our existence, including consciousness. But it takes into account the fact that in the process of evolution the way a creature functions above a certain level of complexity is more than the sum of each individual part working on its own. An organism functions as a whole and this gives it new capacities. Furthermore, there are certain critical thresholds in evolution where once-latent capacities come into operation. One of these thresholds is the emergence of consciousness in human beings.[14] Once this had happened, the human ability to predict consequences and so take steps to safeguard and improve life meant that humans fairly quickly became dominant over other creatures. On this view consciousness serves a vital function and though integrally related to the brain in this life, cannot simply be reduced to it. Our conscious thoughts, hopes and choices play their part in a complex network of causality and may themselves trigger movements in the brain.

As John Habgood has pointed out, explanations of how and why things happen should not be confined to the description of a simple chain of events, as when a vase is knocked over and broken. Most events have complex multiple causes. Why did I catch a cold? Because there was a virus about; because I had been overworking and was tired; because I travelled in a train full of people sneezing; because I had been living on a poor diet. There may be a hundred different causes, some of which will be of the kind 'a virus got into my body'; another of the kind 'I was run down'. In references to 'top-down causation' it is causes of the latter kind, the influence of the whole on the parts, which are in view.[15]

As Habgood goes on to say:

because the brain is such a plastic organ, constantly making new internal connections between nerve fibres or reinforcing or inhibiting old ones and because there is strong evidence that higher mental activities involve the brain as a whole rather than any particular part of it, it might be considered the example *par excellence* of the way

18

in which emergent properties can affect the operation of the parts from which they emerged. Consciousness, in other words, really does make a difference. It is the tapping into, and attending to, all that our human environment has given us, and opening out of the human organism towards new realms of possibility.

If we take this view, we will reject a reductionist materialism, but what are we to make of traditional language of the soul? Can we any longer talk meaningfully of God creating the soul immediately, as though there is a separate spiritual reality related, however integrally, to the body? What we know is that the 'I', our centre of consciousness, our capacity to reflect and choose, emerges at a particular stage, both in evolution itself and in the development of the individual life. This *is* the soul, if you like. But it has not been created separately. It has emerged at a particular point, even if it was latent and potentially there before. This is what Keith Ward calls 'the soft materialists' view', on which

> the soul originates and develops as the brain does, and its proper form of being is to bring to consciousness the properties of the material world in which it is embodied, and to shape those properties in accordance with reflectively formulated goals, rooted in the natural desires and behaviours of the physical organism.[16]

This, we might argue, is very much in accord with the biblical view, which sees human beings not as souls trapped in bodies but as psychosomatic unities: body, mind and spirit bound together in an integral whole. As Genesis 2.7 puts it, 'The LORD God formed man of dust from the ground and breathed into his nostrils the breath of life; and man became a living being' (NASB).

This does not mean that language about the soul has become otiose. Soul language safeguards some fundamental truths about what it is to be a human being. First, that we have an inescapable spiritual dimension, an orientation towards God, and second, that God is immortal and desires us to share his immortality. Some may also want to retain the concept of God creating each soul immediately as a way of safeguarding two other truths. First of all that each human being is unique, not just a result of his or her parents' genes, and second that he or she is not just a material reality but a truly emergent entity, carrying new properties of understanding and intentionality. Each person has a unique individuality and is capable of existing without the actual physical brain each of us has at the moment, though it is a natural part of each person's perfection to be embodied in a public world of interacting persons, and that applies in whatever state lies beyond death as it does now. And, since persons are essentially capable of conscious relationship to God, it is rational to hope that God will cause them to exist in a form in which such a relationship can be properly actualized.[17]

According to the Catholic Catechism, God creates each soul immediately and the general teaching of the Church is that the language of persons and souls is applicable from the moment that the ovum is fertilized. I have suggested that if we look at life in developmental terms, both evolution of life on earth and the unfolding of the individual person, then we should think of consciousness, and hence the soul, as an emerging entity, rooted in the brain and on this earth dependent upon it, yet also inhabiting a rational and spiritual realm of genuine freedom. But at what point does this consciousness arise? And what status should be accorded to the emerging entity before its emergence? Here we move from the language of persons and souls to that of embryos. That takes us back to the earlier discussion in this chapter and forward to the next chapter on abortion. But there is more to be said here about souls.

As argued above, a modern starting point must be that of the book of Genesis and most of the Hebrew Bible, which treats

20

the human person as a unity of body, mind and spirit – what today we term a psychosomatic unity. The soul is not a separate spiritual entity inside the mind or the body, but a dimension of the total person. What the word soul indicates therefore is that an essential feature of what it is to be a human being is that we are orientated towards God and are called into a relationship with him, now and for ever. From this point of view any idea of our souls pre-existing our bodies has to be dismissed. There is no soul without a body, whether a body of flesh and blood or what St Paul termed the spiritual body of the resurrection. Nor can there be any question of believing the Aristotelian view of delayed ensoulment, on which the soul enters the body at a certain stage. Nevertheless, the Aristotelian view, taken into Christianity by Aquinas, did express a valid truth, namely that we should talk about the soul only after a certain period of development of the foetus in the womb, 40 days in the case of men. This we note, is not the stage at which we can talk about a person, if the word person is defined in the Lockean sense of a rational being. But it is the stage at which the foetus is beginning to become responsive – responsive to stimuli, and in particular responsive to the mother in whose womb it lies.

It should not be thought that taking this psychosomatic view of the human person leads inevitably to unbelief in a life beyond death. In fact the distinctive Christian idea is not that of the immortal soul, which had to be fitted rather uneasily into Christian eschatology, but that of the resurrection of the body. When we die all that we are seems to come to an end. But the person we truly are is known to God, who has willed in his goodness to recreate us in a form appropriate to an eternal form of existence. We have no idea what form this will take, but as Christians we die with trust in the Father of Jesus and with hope on the basis of his resurrection and his promise.

In his poem on the resurrection, Gerard Manley Hopkins put it in these words:

In a flash, at a trumpet crash,
I am all at once what Christ is, since he was what I am, and
This Jack, joke, poor potsherd, patch, matchwood, immortal
diamond,
Is immortal diamond.[18]

We can look at human beings from many different points
of view. We are a strange mixture of the physical and the
spiritual, the mortal and the immortal. We are as fragile
and passing as potsherd, patch and matchwood. But all the
time each of us is also immortal diamond, a person being
shaped towards God and for God. In the end, this is what we
are called to be and what through Christ we can be. When all
else has served its purpose and falls away, we are immortal
diamonds.

'The person we truly are is known to God', I wrote above.
That person is known only in part to us, but to be a person at
all, must at least be partly known. To be a person we must have
some degree of consciousness and awareness of ourselves as a
person. According to Locke, a person 'has reason and reflection,
and considers itself as itself, the same thinking thing, in different times and different places'.

Clearly an embryo does not have this capacity, nor indeed
do foetuses or very young infants. Does this mean that they
have no capacity for eternal life? Here I think it is useful to
draw on what I mentioned earlier, the capacity to respond. That
response may not be a conscious one, as it is in us, but there
may still be a response of some kind. It may be that God draws
into his eternal life all that can respond to him in some way,
however inchoately. It is only souls, that is, human persons who
have the capacity to make a conscious response, who can enter
into an eternal relationship with God. But that does not preclude God drawing to himself all that will respond, much as
plants grow up towards the light without knowing that they
do so. All this is highly speculative and beyond the scope of

this little book. The point of considering it at all here is, first, that it emphasizes that a psychosomatic understanding of what it is to be a human being does not mean that essential features of traditional Christian belief have necessarily to be jettisoned. Second, it highlights the fact that the capacity to respond, and not just the capacity to consciously reflect and respond, is a feature to be respected and taken into account in any consideration of the status of the early embryo and the foetus, even if that responsiveness is not enough in itself to be recognized as a feature of personhood.

That capacity to respond in the human embryo has the potential to become a fully conscious response. But, as was argued earlier, potential in itself does not confer rights. Some of the scientific possibilities that are now opening up indicate how precarious it would be to base the granting of rights to what has the potential to become something. For it may be possible in the future to take the cell of a human body and de-differentiate it back to become an embryonic cell, as it were to wind the clock back. Then it would be possible for that embryonic cell to specialize or differentiate into every possible cell of the human body. In other words, if set in the right environment, it could become a human individual and eventually a person. In short, if this scientific possibility was realized every cell in the human body would become a potential person.[19]

Those who are opposed to IVF in general, and to research involving embryos in particular, sometimes base their arguments less on moral philosophy or the tradition of the Church and more on theological considerations derived from the Bible. One expression of this is the appeal to a number of psalms which look to the God who made us and looks after us even from our time in the womb. Another is the fact that if we believe in the incarnation, there was a time when the Eternal Son of God was an embryo in Mary's womb. These are entirely proper expressions of a Christian belief that God has us in mind from the earliest stage of our existence, and even before, but it casts no light on the question of when that existence begins. What these psalms highlight, so often in such a moving manner, is that as human beings we have an inescapable spiritual vocation and destiny. We are called, as unified persons, into a conscious relationship with the eternal God who, we might say, has us in mind from all eternity. We give thanks for his providential care in our lives from even before we were born, trust him now and put our hope in him for the future. This is a vocation, a calling; and more particularly a calling to grow into full personhood, one which reflects the triune God.

Designer babies?

One of the most important advances in recent years has been PGD, preimplantation genetic diagnosis. This involves letting the embryo develop to about the eight-cell stage and then performing a biopsy with one of the cells, to test it for a specific condition or range of conditions. So, for example, if the parents know that they are carriers for cystic fibrosis, and they want to ensure that they have a child who is not born with this debilitating disease, which leads to an early death, they can have their embryos tested and ensure that only an embryo which does not have the condition is implanted. Cystic fibrosis is an obvious example, because it is a single-gene condition that results in a very serious illness. Over the last ten years the number of conditions which can be tested for has grown to 131, many of them extremely rare, with 11 centres licensed to perform the tests.

PGD is strictly regulated by the HFEA. If a clinic in consultation with the patient wishes to undergo this procedure, then an application has to be made to the Authority, and it is then considered by its licence committee. Once PGD for a particular condition has been authorized, and provided the clinic is licensed to undertake PGD, it does not have to reapply every time. On the HFEA website is a list of the main conditions for which licences have so far been granted.

Obviously PGD raises a number of questions. One is about its safety and long-term effects. Removing one cell of an eight-cell organism is a serious procedure. But so far there is no evidence that babies that have come about as a result of this procedure have suffered in any way. The trouble is that the procedure is so new that no long-term studies have yet been possible, so there must still remain a question. All we can say is that so far there is no evidence that the procedure has harmful effects.

Provided that PGD does not raise safety questions in the long term, I cannot see that in itself it poses ethical questions that are not implied by IVF itself. The purpose of IVF is to help the couple conceive. PGD helps them to conceive a healthy baby. It does nature's work in a more conscious way.

There has however been some disquiet from people with disabilities that selecting embryos to avoid the birth of babies who will have handicaps expresses a negative attitude to them. They point out that if such techniques had been employed when the embryo from which they grew first came into existence, they would not be here at all. Some members of the deaf community have gone even further than this, arguing that they should be allowed to select an embryo that will grow up to be a deaf child. This is forbidden under the 2009 Act.

Christians in particular would hope to show sensitivity to people with any kind of disability. However, we do what we can to stop babies being born with HIV without in any way implying a lack of respect or compassion for those suffering with the disease. Indeed the whole of medicine is based on the assumption that disease impairs people's lives; this in no way undermines our belief that people who are actually sick should be helped and cherished. What matters is that society should do all it can to reduce both the functional disadvantages and the stigma of disability. If society has a positive attitude to those with disabilities, then PGD or screening programmes to try to ensure that only healthy children are born will have no adverse effect on those now living with disability.[20]

That said, a number of questions arise in relation to the implications and possibilities posed by PGD. If we allow PGD for serious diseases, what counts as serious? What other factors should be taken into account? Does it matter if the disease strikes early in a person's life, or in adulthood as it does with late onset conditions such as Huntington's? Or if treatments are available? Or if there is only a 40 per cent chance of inheriting it? To take just one example that has recently been considered by the HFEA, concerning the genes labelled BRCA1 and BRCA2, which give rise to a significant risk of breast cancer, and in some cases to ovarian cancer. The cancer might develop in the individual's thirties or forties, there are treatments available such as surgery and radiotherapy, and the penetrance – the likelihood of the disease developing in someone with the gene – is about 80 per cent for breast cancer and 40 per cent for ovarian cancer. A type of colon cancer which is 80 per cent penetrant was also considered. The Authority decided that these were serious conditions with significant risk, and their perception as such by the patient would give rise to a great deal of anxiety. They should therefore in principle be licensable for PGD.

It is even the case that some sex selection is justified under the ordinary rules governing PGD, because there are serious genetic conditions which manifest themselves only in offspring of one sex, usually boys. But what about sex selection for social reasons rather than medical ones? Supposing a family has had five boys and is longing for a girl. Should they be allowed to make that choice through the use of PGD? A few years ago the HFEA held a major public consultation on this and concluded that it should not be permitted. The government reaffirmed that position and the 2008 Act forbids sex selection for social reasons. This is, I think, one of those issues where the right of the individual to choose is outweighed by the potential cost of those choices to society as a whole. There is nothing wrong with a couple wanting a child of a particular sex and they may have perfectly good reasons for doing so. But if it was allowed in principle, that is, was available for anyone, there could be a social cost. We know that in some parts of the world women are devalued and female babies are aborted. Some people would choose to have a child of one sex rather than the other for trivial reasons. Furthermore it could result in an imbalance in the population, whereas at the moment nature keeps the balance between males and females about right.

Then there are issues surrounding the whole idea of what are popularly called designer babies. We could, partly though PGD, but perhaps more effectively through the genetic manipulation of the early embryo, bring about babies of a particular height or colour, or with particular physical or mental characteristics. These possibilities might lead us to make a distinction between treatment to ensure that a medical condition is not passed on and taking steps to enhance particular features of a person. This distinction is not quite as clear-cut as we might like. After all, we could argue that wanting a child to develop a good brain or a good physique was just as important as not wanting it to be born with a particular medical condition. But there are strong arguments against the idea of designing children with particular characteristics. One is that the characteristics which were thought desirable would very much reflect the values of a particular society at a particular time, and those values might be distorted.

In any case, though, it will not be practical to use these techniques to enhance characteristics until a very long way in the future, if it ever becomes possible at all. Most of our features or characteristics involve multiple genes, not just one, and they are likely to have multiple causes, not just one or a few. But there is clearly a danger here that needs to be watched. For if it did become possible it would be easy for people to follow fashion and design babies that conformed to a particular social model, which might or might not be a sound one. Then there is always the nightmare scenario depicted by Kazuo Ishiguro in his novel *Never Let Me Go* of people being bred solely to serve the needs of those in power in society by supplying them with organ transplants late in life. But put all this aside for the moment. What we actually have is the scientific knowledge and skill to stop children being born with debilitating conditions, and that must be something to rejoice in. As Robert Winston has put it:

> It is quite difficult to understand why such a meal is made of the ethics of pre-implantation diagnosis. Screening an embryo for defects is what nature does herself all the time. Although so many human embryos are abnormal, very few abnormal babies are actually born, because most of these embryos perish at the earliest stage of development.[21]

Science simply makes this process more precise and effective. Robert Winston, who is so distinguished in this field, records in his book his dismay at certain attitudes to his work. One peer in the House of Lords debate, for example, said that PGD 'reduced human dignity'. But what makes him feel it is all worth while is the kind of remark made by one patient of his who suffered from an inheritable disease. She went to him for PGD to ensure that she only had male babies, who would not carry her disease. She wanted, she said, 'my children to have more dignity than I have had'.[22]

There is one other aspect of these scientific advances to be considered, and that is the selection of an embryo whose tissue will match that of an ailing brother or sister, so that in due course bone marrow cells, for example, could be taken and used to renew those of the sick child: so-called 'saviour siblings'. The first case to come before the HFEA involved a family who already had a child who was very sick and likely to die of a genetic disorder. The family wanted another child, and they wanted to ensure that this child did not suffer from the same disease. At the same time this child would provide tissue that matched that of the sick sibling. In this case it was possible to argue that PGD and tissue typing (the process whereby the tissue of the baby to be born is tested to ensure its compatibility with that of the sick sibling) were primarily for the benefit of the child who was to be born. It was in the best interest of the child to ensure that it was born free of the disease.

However, in another case that came before the Authority the illness from which the sibling was suffering was not a genetic condition. In this case, could it be argued that the PGD and tissue typing were in the interest of the child to be born, or was it being treated merely as a means to an end, instrumentally, for the sake of the sibling? The HFEA changed its mind on this one, first of all arguing that PGD should not be allowed and then arguing that it should. In its response to the parliamentary select committee considering an early stage of the bill that was to become law as the 2009 Act, the government agreed that in principle the new Authority should be allowed to license such procedures, and to do so not just for life-threatening conditions but for other serious ones.[23] I support that position for the following reasons.

First of all, the reasons why parents have children are likely to be complex and mixed. It is quite possible to imagine parents both wanting another child and at the same time wanting that child to possess tissue that could prevent another of their children from dying. Second, a child born into a family in which its tissue had proved a life-saver, would, it seems to me, have an even more precious place in the family as a result. Far from being regarded as a means to an end, the child would be particularly valued. Suppose, on the other hand, PGD with tissue typing had not taken place and the other child had died. The baby born later would always be in danger of being seen as a replacement for the one who had died, and who might have been saved.

Separate issues of course arise once the child has been born. If its tissue is required later in life, and it is not old enough to give consent itself, the courts have to make the decision, and in doing so they will have to decide whether donation is in the child's best interests. While this might be plausible for a relatively minor procedure like bone marrow donation, it is very unlikely that a court would decide that donation of a solid organ was in a child's best interests.

Breaking the nexus

The old song says that love and marriage go together like a horse and carriage. You could also add that they go together with children. Or, to put it all together, that love leads to marriage and this is expressed in sexual intercourse, which leads to the woman becoming pregnant, the birth of a child and children who are brought up by their parents, namely the couple who first fell in love. What has happened so dramatically over the last decades is that this nexus, which has held in principle for the whole of human history, has been broken.

It was first broken with the advent of reliable contraception, particularly the pill, which was first widely used in the 1960s. Before reliable contraception there was a good chance that sexual intercourse would lead to pregnancy. Since then most intercourse has been for reasons other than to produce children. The Roman Catholic Church still officially teaches that every act of intercourse must be open to the possibility that pregnancy will occur. Non-Catholics and a good many individual Catholics do not accept this.[24] They believe people should make a responsible decision about when to try for children.

Although sperm donation has gone on since the nineteenth century, since the 1960s the nexus has been broken in more dramatic ways:

1 IVF, as the name implies, means that eggs can be fertilized and a woman become pregnant without an act of intercourse occurring. It happens through medical manipulation and without a physical union.[25]
2 Sperm and egg donation means that the couple can have children whose genetic connection is with only one parent.

Either the egg or the sperm comes from someone else altogether. In 1992, for example, 22 eggs were donated and by 2004 this had grown to 408. Since 1991 there have been 1,700 births (or 2,000 children, because some births produced twins) from donated egg or sperm.

3 Surrogacy means that a couple can have children without the woman becoming pregnant. Someone else altogether will go through pregnancy on behalf of the couple, with either a donated egg or that of the mother who wishes to have a child but who is unable to bear the child herself.

4 It is possible now for a woman past the age of menopause to have a child. There have been a number of highly publicized cases in the last few years of women in their sixties having a child. Since the woman is no longer able to produce her own eggs, someone else's egg is fertilized and implanted in her womb. In the future such pregnancies may be possible with the woman's own eggs, which will have been taken from her and frozen at an earlier stage in her life.

5 It is possible for a single woman or a same-sex couple to have children. In the case of two women this means that the one bearing the child will have used donated sperm. In the case of two men, it will mean one of them donating sperm to a woman, who will have agreed to bear a child for them.

6 There are other scientific possibilities in the pipeline. For example, it might prove possible to take a cell from a woman and de-differentiate it, as it were rewind it, to obtain an embryonic stem cell, and then produce male sperm from this which could be used to fertilize a woman partner.

Each of these procedures, either in existence now or a possibility for the future, poses separate ethical questions. But there is one theme that runs through them all – the ability to choose. What distinguishes all of them is the way our human choices have opened up or multiplied. The old nexus has been broken not just in one place, as with reliable contraception, but all along the line.

Many of the procedures outlined in the preceding list strike people as shocking, particularly those of us who have been brought up in a socially conservative environment. The main difference is that in contrast to society 50 years ago, there is now an overriding emphasis on the importance of individual choice. So let us look at this.

The underlying assumption behind the breaking of the nexus is that people should be free to choose. So why should their choice not be respected? If an infertile man wants a child, why should not he and his partner seek a sperm donor? If a sterile woman cannot produce eggs or eggs of the right quality, why should she, with the agreement of her partner, not be free to seek an egg donor? If a woman cannot bear a child because of a defective womb, why should she not find a surrogate to do it for her? If a single person or a same-sex couple want children, why should they be denied this? If a woman who is past the menopause wants a child and can find some means of doing so, why should she be denied what she most wants?

These are genuine questions. But they need to be put in that particular way. In short, there needs to be a good reason or good reasons why such people should be denied what they say they want. Or to put it another way, why should I, or society, impose choices on others? Unless there is good reason, it constitutes bullying or tyranny. As in the chapter on end-of-life issues, I would argue here that personal choice cannot be the only consideration, for why should we value choice unless it is set in a wider moral framework in which choice is an important moral component? If we value choice and choice alone, it remains purely arbitrary from a moral point of view.

One good reason why people should not be given their choice is that the choice would lead to harmful consequences of which they may not be fully aware at the time. This is why continuing research is so important. It is only good research that can show whether people's fears are well- or ill-founded, and whether their criticisms of a particular practice are based on evidence. For example, some people feel that children brought up by same-sex couples will suffer in various ways as a result. But research does not bear this out. A number of studies in the 1970s and 1980s on the children of lesbian mothers did not show any likelihood of psychological disorder or difficulty in forming relationships with their peers. More recently, studies on children now in their early or mid-twenties who were brought up by lesbian mothers showed a similar result. One criticism is that people brought up in this way are more likely to become lesbian or homosexual themselves. But of the 25 people studied only two were homosexual. The argument that those brought up by same-sex couples are more likely themselves to be of a similar sexual orientation is in any case thoroughly specious, as the vast majority of lesbian and gay people were born to and brought up by heterosexual couples.

Another example of valuable research is that done on children brought up as a result of surrogacy arrangements – either partial, when a surrogate mother provides the egg, or full, when the couple who want children provide a fertilized egg and IVF is used before implantation in the surrogate mother's womb. Robert Winston, despite having a very early experience of helping a patient receive this form of treatment, said he had many questions and doubts about the difficulties that could arise. But research has now laid his doubts to rest. The latest study by Professor Susan Golombok in 2006, building on her earlier work, compared 34 surrogacy families with 41 donor insemination families, 41 oocyte (sperm or egg) donation families and a control group of normally conceived children and their parents. They found no difference in psychological well-being between the various groups and no disadvantage in those where there was no gestational link with the child. A high percentage of the families who had received assistance in reproducing their children had informed them of this by a fairly early age.

It is sometimes claimed that our current emphasis on choice expresses an unjustified assumption that people have a right to something, and that this is part of an unhealthy culture of entitlement. This is not necessarily the case. A whining sense of entitlement, or a resentful sense of having a right to something, are indeed not very attractive. But it is quite possible for a person to recognize with great intensity that having a child is a gift, not an entitlement, and still believe that his or her choice should be respected. Indeed, if such a person has tried for a long time to have children without success and eventually, through various scientific procedures, succeeds, then he or she is likely to feel even more strongly that any children who are born are indeed gifts. No one has a right to a child, because children are a precious gift, but women do have a right to try for a child. That is the point.

There are three ways in which the primacy of individual choice might be overridden: if there is a risk to health, if such a choice conflicts with religious conviction or if it is in conflict with the wider good of society. The first and most obvious is if the physician thinks the health of the mother or the resulting child would be at risk. As Robert Winston has put it:

> I believe my overriding duty, as a fertility specialist, was to assist pregnancies with maximum concern for the welfare of mother and child. I might have refused treatment if I thought the health of either would be seriously at risk. I might have refused treatment if I had grounds to believe that the well-being of any resulting child would be seriously at risk. In all other circumstances, I would respect the right of women to try to have children.[26]

Then there are some people who accept that if they follow a particular religion faithfully, some or all of the procedures outlined above are not open to them. The Roman Catholic Church offers the obvious example of this.

The primacy given to personal choice is a feature of liberal democratic societies whose roots lie in the seventeenth century. It is sometimes thought, because religions have often opposed it, that personal choice is a secular value. On the contrary, those who first championed it, like John Locke, or before him, the left-wing elements in Cromwell's forces, were Christians. Moreover, how can Christians, who believe we have been endowed by God with free choice, a capacity which God himself respects, in any way downplay it?[27]

Such a stress on the importance of free choice should not be confused with individualism, or individualistic views of humanity. Mind, as Austin Farrer used to say, is a social reality. We are talked into talking by others and then learn to do that talking in our heads that we call thinking; we become and remain human persons only in and through our relationships with other persons. We are essentially social beings. But that in no way detracts from each of us having our choices respected within the totality of the communities and societies to which we belong. This means, of course, that our choices will have to be considered in relation to the effect they may have on the health and well-being of those societies. Furthermore, though this is more controversial, society itself, through its major institutions, will not be value free or neutral. It will be the product of a particular history and culture, including its religion. This factor too needs to be taken into account, as Edmund Burke so eloquently argued. But even if we have an organic view of society like Burke, as political conservatives tended to do until the late twentieth century, this does not in itself contradict the moral importance of respecting individual choice unless there is convincing reason not to do so. People who get married and choose to plan a family in the ordinary way have their choice respected. Exactly the same respect should be accorded those who are not able to do this and who use IVF or some related technique.

Finally, however, for those who are not in that position, then what must be considered is the effect of granting certain choices on the welfare and well-being of society as a whole. Are there harmful consequences of any or all of these options now open to people who want to have children? If so, such consequences must be taken into account and weighed against the very serious step of denying certain people what they most want. This method of arguing, classically brought to the fore by Utilitarians in the nineteenth century, has sometimes been disparaged by religious people, who see ethics more in terms of actions being right or wrong without taking consequences into account. But while there is a place for a moral law which regards actions as being right or wrong in themselves, the weighing up of consequences is a fundamental factor in most decision making, and is absolutely basic when it comes to the formation of social policy and the making of laws.

Each of the procedures mentioned above raises questions and they have been and still are the subject of much debate. What has resulted is a system of regulation which recognizes that there might be a social cost to this emphasis on the primacy of choice and which therefore sets up an ethical and legal framework in which it is to be exercised. This has been legislated for by Parliament and is regulated by the HFEA. To take one example, that of sperm donation. If this is allowed, what is to stop one man becoming the father of thousands of children with the risk that in the future half-siblings will marry one another? Regulatory policy has taken this into account and so there is a legal limit of ten families of which an individual sperm donor can be the genetic father. Or, to take another example, what is to stop a woman in desperate financial need selling her eggs and so opening the way to poor women being exploited for their bodies? The answer is the law, which allows expenses and loss of earnings only up to a relatively small amount for both sperm and egg donation. This is a contentious issue and there are those who argue that people should be able to sell their sperm or eggs. So far the HFEA has resisted such arguments and I believe there are sound reasons for so doing.

There are two other general factors to consider in addition to this current emphasis on the primacy of personal choice, one which reinforces that priority and one which causes us to hesitate.

The reinforcing factor is that people who have tried by natural methods to have a child and not succeeded, and who seek assisted reproduction to do so, are people who really want children. People who put themselves through medical procedures that are invasive and can be uncomfortable, in order to have children, whether they are married, single or in a same-sex relationship, are again people who show by this that they really want children. A child who comes into the world truly wanted has been given a very good start.

Child psychologists say that what really matters for the development of a child is the quality of the relationship between that child and its mother, or mother substitute. It is this bonding and loving relationship which more than anything else shapes the child's sense of his or her own value. As potential parents we have inherited a strong cultural disposition to think that it is important to have 'our' children, that is children who inherit a mixture of the genes of both father and mother. I do not want to knock that. It is a natural inclination with social consequences. Indeed we recognize the importance of the genetic factor in the way that donor anonymity has been abolished in the UK and it will now be legally possible for offspring conceived by donor since 2005, once they reach the age of 18, to discover the identity of their genetic parents. But if it is the quality of the relationship between the growing child and those bringing it up that really matters, the question of where a person's genes come from cannot be the overriding consideration.

The note of hesitation and caution arises from what I term nature's accumulated wisdom. In very round figures, the universe has been in existence nearly 13.6 billion years, the earth some four billion and life on earth about four million. In short we are the product of a long, complex, costly process of evolution. The processes which nature has 'devised' to ensure that our species reproduces itself have been tried and tested in difficult circumstances, over a very long period. It works, otherwise you and I would not be in existence. There is here an accumulated wisdom which we should respect and take seriously. One of the great lessons that we began to learn in the 1960s, when it was found that the extensive use of pesticides could be highly damaging, is that unlimited scientific ingenuity can damage and destroy delicate ecological systems. Since then we have been aware of this lesson in a range of other ways, above all with regard to the crisis over climate change. This is not an argument for stopping scientific advances or always taking the most traditional course. But it is an argument for what in some spheres is now called the precautionary principle, that is, being cautious about our interventions in natural processes. There may be unintended consequences. This is an argument that I also touch on in the chapter on end-of-life issues.

One concern that has emerged from this kind of consideration is the effect of inter-generational donation. This can be of two kinds. As an example of the first kind, a young woman has had treatment for cancer and is not able to produce any eggs of her own, so her mother donates one of her eggs to her. The resulting child will be the genetic daughter of her grandmother, and her social mother will also be her genetic sister. The other example is the reverse of this. A woman wishes to start a second family with a new partner, but is not able to produce her own eggs, so a daughter from her first marriage donates an egg to her. The resulting child will be both her social daughter and her genetic granddaughter.

Various questions arise here. Can consent in such donations be genuinely free and without pressure? This pressure need not

be wilful. It might arise simply from the nature of the relationship. For example, the daughter in the first case might still be
financially dependent on the mother. Then there is the issue
of confusion of relationships, and whether a child growing up
with this mixture of cross-generational social and genetic
relationships would not have a somewhat confused identity.
And, more widely, there is the social issue of consanguinity and
the forbidden degrees of relationship. In law certain kinds of
relationship are forbidden, for good medical reasons, because
of the fear of exploitation of younger members of the family
and the desirability of certain fixed familial structures in
society. More is involved than simply letting one member of
a family help another out. There are wider consequences to
be considered. This does not mean that inter-generational
donation should always be ruled out, but it does mean that
personal choice cannot be the only consideration.

The long-term consequences and the long-term impact
on society are of particular importance in relation to genetic
modification of the human embryo, which at the moment is
forbidden by law except for research purposes. This is not an
argument for never doing it, but it is the flashing of a warning
light on the grounds of possible consequences in the long
term.

So the position taken here is that the primacy of individual
choice should be supported in principle. There need to be com-
pelling reasons to do with the health of the mother and the
resulting children, or of society as a whole, if it is to be overridden. In the field of reproduction, those who seek assistance
will be people who genuinely want children, and that is likely
to give them a very good start in life. Furthermore, it is the
quality of the relationship between the child and those bringing
it up that is the truly important factor. If there are social
consequences of these choices, these can be, and have been,
managed through appropriate laws and regulatory action. But
of course this is an area that needs to be kept under continual

41

scrutiny. That said, nature's accumulated wisdom is not to be ignored, and we cannot assume that every advance which can be done scientifically should be pursued.

Meanwhile, the fact that thousands of women who very much wanted children have been able to have them, as a result of IVF and associated techniques made possible by modern medical science, is something for which to be profoundly thankful.

Embryo research

Research on the early embryo was permitted in the original 1990 Act but, as I mentioned earlier, the purposes for which it was allowed were expanded in 2002 to include serious diseases. Earlier there had to be a direct connection between the purpose of the research and enabling healthy babies to be born.[28] With the 2002 regulations that connection was broken. This expansion was controversial. Whereas until that point the research could in some sense be seen to be in the interest of the embryo, with the new purposes relating to serious disease the research would be for the benefit of other people. It is basic to the moral outlook of most people that we do not treat others merely as means to an end, making them instruments of some other purpose. Hence the unease about the expansion of the reasons for which research may be done. Most people would find the idea of experimenting on babies or foetuses in the womb to find cures for other people morally repugnant. All decent people believe that the Nazis were totally immoral to carry out experiments on adults without their informed consent. But here we are talking about the very early embryo, and this raises again the question of its status. If we were dealing with a human person then that research would indeed be immoral, and that is the view of the Roman Catholic Church and some other people. But it is basic to my own involvement and the whole argument of this book that the early embryo, though it is to be treated with respect, is not a human individual, for the reasons set out in earlier pages. We have here a potential individual, and the question is whether instrumentalizing that potential individual somehow degrades human beings. Not, in my view, if it is done for serious reasons which may bring about real benefits for those who are suffering.

Although some embryos are created specially for research, the vast majority of research is carried out on embryos that would otherwise be destroyed. As Professor Gordon Dunstan, the most distinguished medical ethicist at the time of the Warnock report and its ensuing debate, has written:

> Upon this waste, medical intervention imposes an economy. If successful it provides a baby where otherwise there would be none. The genetic information stored in the cells can be read; what is thus learned can be ordered into knowledge; knowledge can be put to beneficial, lifesaving use. The argument is *not* that because nature is prodigal we may be prodigal; because so much life or potential life is lost, one more does not matter. It is the reverse. It is that nature's prodigality is turned to creative use; natural loss is lessened, albeit to a minute degree.[29]

One of the reasons why scientists were very anxious to have the 2002 regulations approved by Parliament was because of the hope held out by cloning. This involves taking the nucleus out of an egg and replacing it with the nucleus of an adult cell (see Figure 1). The resulting cells of the fertilized egg begin to divide and develop in the usual way and when the eight-day stage has been reached, the inner mass of the blastocyst, as it is termed at that point, consisting of about 100 cells, is removed, put in a special solution and allowed to continue dividing. The cells thus dividing and replicating are called embryonic stem cells and their importance resides in the fact that under appropriate conditions they can develop and differentiate into any of the specialist cells of the human body; hence they are called pluripotent. Furthermore, the stem cell line formed by extracting the inner mass of the blastocyst will go on and on indefinitely.

The reason why medical scientists are so excited about this technique is that it may offer real hope to people suffering from a range of serious and debilitating diseases: Alzheimer's,

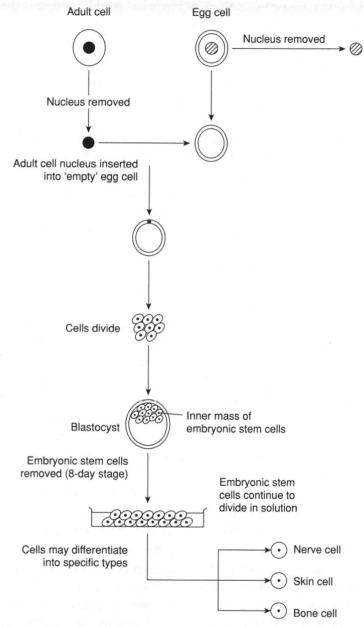

Figure 1 The cloning process

Parkinson's, diabetes and so on. For what could happen is that the nucleus from the cell of someone suffering from such a disease would replace the nucleus of an egg, as described above, and a stem cell line would be formed. This stem cell line, coming from the sufferer, would be compatible with his or her own cells and could in principle be made to specialize in such a way that damaged cells could be replaced or renewed. The key point is that the cells would not be rejected by the body because they were that body's own cells, or from a stem cell line that was compatible with that body's cells.

It is important to note that realization of this hope is likely to be a long way in the future and there are many hurdles to overcome. It is also important to be aware that other kinds of cells are already being used to treat people, adult stem cells such as those from bone marrow, which come from the body, not the destruction of an embryo, and which therefore do not give rise to any ethical problems. These too hold out hope. The difference is that adult stem cells are already specialist in their operation and there are likely to be limits as to their use. Hence they are termed multipotent, able to replace a limited number of cells, not every one of them in the body like the pluripotent cells that come from embryos.

The House of Lords Select Committee on Stem Cells concluded as a result of extensive consultations with scientists working in the field at that time that research was needed on both adult stem cells and embryonic stem cells, because at that stage it was impossible to tell which was going to be most fruitful, or for what kinds of disease.[30]

The debates in the House of Lords both prior to and after the report of the select committee focused on whether it was really necessary to have embryonic stem cells, or whether adult stem cells were all that is necessary both for research and treatment. There is no doubt that adult stem cells are already vital in some forms of treatment but, as indicated above, they are multipotent rather than pluripotent, that is, they can replace only specific types of cell. Furthermore, for research purposes, which is all that is legally authorized at the moment, embryonic stem cells are essential in order to discover what happens in the process of development from the earliest stage.

Since those debates there has been a further scientific advance, and we now have the ability to produce pluripotent cells without the use of an embryo at all. A single cell is taken from an embryo (which can be done without destroying it, as in the case with biopsies for PGD), and this cell can be induced into producing more cells capable of differentiating into any cell in the human body. Hence the name which has been given to this type of cell, induced pluripotent cells.

The word 'cloning' as applied to research has given rise to unnecessary fears. By cloning, some people think of the above technique being used to produce an embryo which will be placed in the womb to produce an exact likeness of the person who has provided the nucleus of his or her adult cell. But this is forbidden by law and is something that no responsible scientist wishes to do. Sometimes the phrase 'therapeutic cloning' is used, to indicate this technique is simply for research with a view to curing people, but even that can give rise to unreasonable fears. The technical name is Cell Nuclear Replacement (CNR), and this is to be preferred.

Where will all this lead? What might come next? Or after that? We have already raised the question of the slippery-slope argument. This kind of argument is sometimes dismissed out of hand, but it should not be. There are slippery slopes, and sometimes we find ourselves sliding down them against our will. For many people the 1967 Act that legalized abortion was one such slope, and I will examine this in the next chapter. Supported at the time by many good people, including many Christians, the Act has unfortunately been so applied that the original carefully defined circumstances in which an abortion might legally be carried out have become almost meaningless, and women who are determined to obtain an abortion will find a way of doing so. So I take the slippery-slope argument seriously. I will consider it again in relation to end-of-life issues. What it means is that if there is a slope, it is vital to have something firm to hold on to so that one does not slide down it out of control. The 1990 Act, as amended by the 2008 Act, does in my view provide such a firm handrail.

The law as laid out in the 2008 Act is quite clear about two things. First, that no research can take place on the early embryo after 14 days, or the formation of the primitive streak, whichever is the earlier. All such embryos have to be destroyed before that point. Second, no early embryo on which research has taken place may be implanted in a woman's womb.

What needs to be noted is that despite the great scientific advances since 1990, with scientists calling for permission for yet another line of research, there has been no serious questioning of this aspect of the legislation. Everyone agrees that the early embryo which has been used for research must not be implanted and must be destroyed. As mentioned earlier, the primitive streak is formed around 14 days, so 14 days has been taken together with the formation of the streak as a clear marker.

So, if there is a fear of a slippery slope, the law in this case provides two handrails to hold on to. First, there is a strict prohibition on the implantation of cloned embryos in the womb, a ban which it would be desirable to obtain internationally. Second, what is allowed at the moment is only research, which can only take place in the first 14 days of development, during which time the early embryo has to be destroyed. In the case of CNR it is destroyed at eight days.

The question of hybrids

Scientific research does not stop, however, and one recent controversial issue considered by Parliament and the HFEA was that of hybrids, embryos created when the genetic material of two species is mixed. Here a distinction needs to be made between cytoplasmic hybrids and true hybrids. The creation of a cytoplasmic hybrid involves the same technique as that already described for CNR, but in this case the nucleus is removed from the cell of an animal, not a human egg. It is then replaced by the nucleus of a human adult cell. It can be made to divide and develop as before and the resulting stem cell line can be used for research.

The reason why some scientists are very anxious to engage with this technique is that at this early experimental stage it takes a huge number of eggs in order to produce even one stem cell line. Female human eggs available for research are relatively few in number but the supply of animal eggs, which can be obtained from abattoirs, is virtually unlimited.

The HFEA concluded that cytoplasmic hybrids are human for the purposes of the Act, and therefore can and must be regulated. Although animal material (the mitochondria of a denucleated animal egg, the mitochondria being the DNA of the outer shell of the egg which supplies energy) is used, the resulting embryo will be 99.9 per cent human and any stem cells extracted will be 100 per cent human.

The creation of a so-called true hybrid is carried out differently. Here human material and animal material, probably a sperm and egg, are fully mixed. The result will be partly human, partly animal. This gives rise to great unease, and conjures up images of Frankenstein's monsters walking the earth. But, once again, we are dealing only with research up to 14 days, with all implantation strictly forbidden by law. Nevertheless, this process raises additional questions to those raised by the ability to carry out CNR with human eggs, or even cytoplasmic hybrids.

One is the feeling that it is wrong to bring together any animal and human material. But we do this already, most obviously with xenotransplants, when for example we might take material, like a valve, from a pig's heart in order to help repair a human heart. It has also been brought home to us just how much genetic material we share with the rest of the animal kingdom. For example, we share 99.4 per cent of our genes with chimpanzees. So the fact of mixing animal and human material cannot in itself be wrong.

But true hybrids go beyond this. It is not merely that their creation involves a mixing of material, but that what we might call the organizing principle of the creature so created will be neither a human nor any known animal but an unknown mixture. It is not just some animal material in a human but a different creature altogether, and this seems to offend our notion that there are different species whose dignity, like our dignity as human beings, needs to be respected. Cats are cats and dogs are dogs, and while we breed within species we do not generally breed between them (except in the case of asses, which come about from horses and donkeys, but who cannot themselves reproduce).

The idea of distinct species which should not be mixed up comes to us from the book of Genesis, where God creates each one separately. In fact we know that each species, including ourselves, is the result of a long period of evolution from earlier ancestors whom we share. The different species were not placed on the earth in a fixed and final form. They have evolved.

But there is something in this argument from the dignity of different species, including ourselves. Our dignity resides not in our bodies, which sometimes seem less than perfectly adapted for the way we are (as those who suffer from persistent back trouble know all too well!), but from our capacity to think and know we are thinking, to choose and know that we are choosing, to love and to pray. It would be very cruel to bring into existence a creature which not only had a grotesque physical appearance by our standards, but which had the rudiments of feeling and self-consciousness. What would it feel and think about itself in relation to us? And how would we treat it? That is a road down which we should not go. Nor will we, so long as regulation holds – and there is no reason to think that it won't. Again, what we are talking about is research up to 14 days, a tiny bundle of multiplying cells, not a creature. So although there are very serious questions about true hybrids, and there are at the moment no scientists pressing to do work on them, there may in the end prove to be no overwhelming reason why research should not be undertaken if this is shown to be necessary for a good purpose.

The ethical and other questions around true hybrids were not discussed by the HFEA before the 2008 bill came to Parliament. The Authority had only discussed, and approved, cytoplasmic hybrids, which were judged to be human, and which therefore at the time fell under the legislation of the 1990 Act. When the issue came before Parliament, however, the government decided to bring in a new term, human admixed embryos, which includes not just cytoplasmic hybrids, but any mixture of human and animal material at the embryonic level which would give rise to an entity which was predominantly human. Again, it must be mentioned that the creation of such material is allowed only for research purposes. Moreover, if an application for research using such human admixed embryos ever came before the HFEA they would have to decide that the proposed research was necessary or desirable, and that it could not be done in any other way.

Developments since the first baby produced with the help of IVF have been truly remarkable, with far-reaching significance. Such advances can initially seem disturbing, and it is right that we should continue to scrutinize them from an ethical point of view. Nevertheless, this chapter has been written in the belief that we should be profoundly grateful for the God-given skills that have enhanced the lives of so many women, and that have the potential to bring better health to millions in the future.

2
ABORTION[1]

The 1967 Act and its consequences

If the argument about embryo research has been contentious, the dispute over the rights and wrongs of abortion has been ferocious. In many countries, especially the United States, it is the most divisive of all public issues. Pro-choice and pro-life lobbies continue to wage fierce campaigns. In the British Parliament the Human Fertilisation and Embryology Bill put forward in 2009 offered a platform for people on both sides of the debate to propose amendments either to tighten or to loosen the law: either to lower the upper threshold for abortion, which at the moment is 24 weeks, or to make it easier for people to obtain an abortion in the early stages of pregnancy.

It surprises many people to know that there is no legal right to have an abortion in the UK. It remains a criminal offence. However, it is not an offence if the abortion is carried out on one or more of the following grounds, as laid out in section 1(1) of the 1967 Abortion Act:

Subject to the provisions of this section, a person shall not be guilty of an offence under the law relating to abortion when a pregnancy is terminated by a registered medical practitioner if two registered medical practitioners are of the opinion, formed in good faith:

(a) that the pregnancy has not exceeded its twenty-fourth week and that the continuance of the pregnancy would involve risk, greater than if the pregnancy were terminated, of injury to the physical or mental health of the pregnant woman or any existing children of her family; or

(b)   that the termination is necessary to prevent grave permanent injury to the physical or mental health of the pregnant woman; or

(c)   that the continuance of the pregnancy would involve risk to the life of the pregnant woman, greater than if the pregnancy were terminated; or

(d)   that there is a substantial risk that if the child were born it would suffer from physical or mental abnormalities as to be seriously handicapped.

(2) In determining whether the continuance of a pregnancy would involve such risk of injury to health as is mentioned in paragraph (a) or (b) of subsection (1) of this section, account may be taken of the woman's actual or reasonably foreseeable environment.[2]

Various specific points are worth noting from the 2008 figure of 195,296 residents who had abortions, the most recent currently available. First, the highest number of abortions were carried out among 19-year-olds, some 36 abortions per 1,000 women pregnant at that age. Second, 90 per cent of abortions were carried out under 13 weeks, and 73 per cent under 10 weeks. Third, the number of abortions carried out in 2008 on ground (d), the possibility of the child being handicapped, was 1,988, about 1 per cent of those performed.

As can be seen from (b), (c) and (d), abortion on some grounds can be carried out at any stage. This was not specified in the original 1967 Act but was incorporated in an amendment in 1990. These late abortions, that is, after 24 weeks, are particularly distressing and receive much publicity, but as a proportion of the whole they make up less than 0.1 per cent, some 124 in 2008.

But it is under category (a) that most abortions are authorized, 98 per cent of the total of the 2008 figure. Of these the vast majority were permitted with reference to the mental health of the mother. Less than 0.5 per cent of those abortions were on the grounds of mothers' physical health. It is this figure of 98 per cent which has given rise to most concern. For as David Steel, the architect of the 1967 Abortion Act, has commented, it is certainly not what he and other supporters of the Act had in mind. The great evil that needed to be remedied at the time was the number of illegal back-street abortions, as a result of which healthy women were dying. Furthermore, it was particularly the poor who were the victims, for the rich could find a way round the law even then.[3] It is a situation well brought out in Mike Leigh's 2004 film *Vera Drake*. In order to stop these unnecessary deaths the supporters of the Act wanted to make it possible for people, especially the poor, with good grounds for an abortion, to obtain one legally. In fact what has happened is that the grounds set out in (a) allow anyone who is determined to obtain a legal abortion to do so. This is because the Royal College of Obstetricians and Gynaecologists recommends that in considering the question of the physical and mental health of the mother attention should be paid to the definition of health used by the World Health Organization, which refers to a person's total health and well-being, not just the absence of disease. Furthermore, pregnancy and childbirth are always more hazardous than an abortion, so it can be argued that the well-being of the mother is best promoted by an abortion, particularly when the physician can take into account 'the woman's actual or reasonably foreseeable environment'.

Recent debate has focused on the issue of whether the upper limit for abortions on ground (a) should be lowered to 22 weeks. The best medical evidence at the moment tells against doing this, because even if some babies can survive at that age the likelihood of severe handicap is high. At the same time other groups are campaigning to make abortion in the first three months easier to obtain by no longer having to obtain the agreement of two doctors. It is argued that it should be possible to have an abortion without the agreement of a doctor, or at least with the agreement of only one.[4]

The pregnant woman's decision

Polly Toynbee, in a recent debate about whether the upper limit for abortions on grounds of (a) should be lowered to 22 weeks, said it was indeed the case that more babies between 22 and 24 weeks can now survive. However, she said, that is not the point: 'Give in to that argument and the case for a woman's supreme right over her own body and destiny is lost. It is handed back again to the doctors and priests and politicians to make those decisions for her.'[5]

Any man writing on the subject of a woman's right to choose an abortion should do so with a great deal of hesitation and humility. It is obvious that it is the woman who has to go through the pregnancy and who still bears the brunt of the upbringing of any children. Quite simply, it is not a male decision. Nevertheless, a good number of feminists do not like the kind of language that Polly Toynbee employs about a woman having a supreme right over her own body. Nor do they like those analogies which liken abortion to a landlord turning out an unwanted tenant, or to a woman who cuts off life support to someone who is totally dependent on her for this.

Pregnancy has also been described in these words:

To be pregnant is to be *inhabited*. It is to be *occupied*. It is to be in a state of physical intimacy of a particularly thorough-going nature. The fetus intrudes on the body massively; whatever medical risks one faces or avoids, the brute fact remains that the fetus shifts and alters the very physical boundaries of the woman's self.[6]

To this Professor Emily Jackson responds:

Of course, the fetus is not a malicious intruder: it is occupying the woman's body through no fault of its own.

However, the claim being made on this line of analysis is that the state does not have the right to force the woman to continue in this relationship of unparalleled intimacy without her consent.[7]

Jackson mentions the issue of consent. A woman may consent to the sexual intimacy which resulted in a pregnancy but this does not of itself mean that she consents to the result. If someone walks down a dark street and is attacked, that person chose to walk that street in the dark but did not consent to being mugged. Such a person may be responsible for an unwise or thoughtless decision but that is different from saying that he or she consents to the consequences of it.

A good way to look at the decision from a woman's point of view is in terms of the responsibility towards that which both is and is not her body. Professor Catharine MacKinnon has written that the foetus is 'More than a body part but less than a person . . . From the standpoint of the pregnant woman, it is both me and not me. It "is" the pregnant woman in the sense that it is in her and of her and is hers more than anyone's. It "is not" her in the sense that she is not all that is there.'[8] She quotes the poet Adrienne Rich: 'The child that I carry for nine months can be defined *neither* as me nor as not-me.'[9]

A woman making the decision about abortion is therefore conscious of her responsibility to herself, to her family if she has one, and to what is at once her and not her. It is not a question of a supreme right to abort the foetus. It is a question of being conscious of a number of claims in relation to which she has to make a responsible choice. In that sense it is indeed her choice and not anyone else's. But this does not mean that no one else, even doctors, priests or politicians, has a voice in the making of that decision. If someone is attempting to commit suicide we try to stop him. Although that person may think it is entirely up to him whether or not he kills himself he is not the only one to have a stake in the decision. His family and friends have a proper concern about it. Wider society has a view on it, as expressed by the fact that helping someone to commit suicide is a criminal offence. Similarly, wider society prevents a woman selling her organs. She may be desperately poor and say it is her right to do what she wants with her own body. But society, through the law, tries to protect her and other vulnerable people by not allowing her to make such a choice.

So, as the quotations from Adrienne Rich and Catharine MacKinnon above indicate so powerfully, the experience of being pregnant, that is, the issue from a woman's perspective, cannot be summed up in the usual polarized way, with a woman's right to do what she wants with her own body being championed on the one hand, and the right of the foetus to be considered as an independent person on the other. It is of course the woman who has in the end to make the decision. But in making that decision there is a claim on her from within her own body. What is the nature and force of that claim?

The foetus from 14 days

It was argued in the previous chapter that the formation of the primitive streak, that is, the first beginnings of the nervous system at about 14 days, is a highly significant point for the moral evaluation of the early embryo. After this, and implantation in the womb, which takes place a little earlier, at about seven or eight days after conception, it is clear we have a human individual; human life that under normal circumstances in the right environment will develop into a feeling, thinking, choosing human being, a person. Does that foetus, that human individual at this very early stage, have the same right to life as a baby and an adult? The Roman Catholic Church and many Evangelicals respond with an unequivocal 'Yes'. Others say that what we have here is still simply a developing organism devoid, until much later, of any capacity to feel pain and without, until later still, even rudimentary consciousness.

The distinguished American philosopher Ronald Dworkin has argued that in so far as we go on seeing the debate in these terms, there will be no meeting of minds and no possibility of any kind of compromise. But, he suggests, the public rhetoric of this debate is highly misleading. What the polls reveal is that people do not in fact see the early embryo in terms of such stark contrasts. He draws a distinction between understanding the foetus as a creature having interests and rights, and regarding it as human life with intrinsic value. On the basis of the first view it is clear that the foetus has an interest in staying alive, and the right to be protected by the state. This is what he calls a derivative right, for it is a right derived from the fundamental conviction that the foetus has interests. In contrast to this there is the view that human life has an intrinsic, innate value; this life is sacred even in its earliest stages, before it has any rights. In this case we recognize the value of that life and acknowledge that the state has a duty to protect it, but this is what he calls a detached view. People may be very strongly opposed to abortion on this basis, but the ground of their objection will be different from that of objections based on the notion that the foetus has interests and rights.

Dworkin believes that the conviction that the foetus has an intrinsic value is likely to be the actual basis for the objection that is felt to abortion. So, for example, most people, even if they take a very conservative position, are in fact willing to allow abortion if the mother's life is directly threatened. But on the first view this is inconsistent, for we cannot say that one person has a greater right to life than another. To kill a foetus, on this view, is to murder someone for the sake of someone else, and we do not allow this in the case of babies or adults, however severely disabled they are.

The terms derivative and detached are not particularly illuminating, and while examining Dworkin's argument I will simply refer to a 'rights-based' view of the foetus and a 'value-based' one. His fundamental assumption behind this distinction is stated in these words: 'It makes no sense to suppose that something has interests of *its own* – as distinct from its being important what happens to it – unless it has, or has had, some form of consciousness: some mental as well as physical life.'[10]

Human life, even in its earliest stages, has an intrinsic value, even though it cannot be said to have interests. We might compare this with the intrinsic value of a great work of art, which does not have any interests, but whose destruction would be a tragedy. Or we can reflect on the loss of a beautiful plant. It is possible to deeply regret the loss of something though it may have no interest of its own in staying alive.

Some argue that the foetus has an interest of its own when pain can be felt. This stage is said to be reached at about 30 weeks, though 26 weeks is often taken as the properly cautious point when this should be taken into account. But it might also be argued that an interest in staying alive only arises when a creature can feel more complex emotions, and that point is more indeterminate.

Others argue that in destroying a foetus you are violating the rights of the person who would have been born if the foetus had not been so destroyed. It is, after all, preventing someone from coming into being – if the foetus that became me had been destroyed, I would not be here now. This is a strongly felt objection when it comes from those with disabilities, who object to foetuses being terminated on the grounds of handicap. But, following Dworkin, it is important to draw a distinction between saying that once a person exists, destroying his or her foetus would have been against that person's interests, and saying that if a foetus is destroyed there is then no one against whose interests this would be. No one was harmed, because there is no one there to be harmed. So, if the person who became my father had run off before his marriage was consummated, I would not be here. But if he had run off in this way, this would not have been against the interests of anyone then living except his wife, for I would not have been born. There was no me whose rights could have been violated.

Dworkin continues that this distinction helps to illuminate the apparent contradiction that although pregnant women are urged not to smoke or do anything else that might hurt the unborn child in their womb, it is nevertheless legally possible to abort that unborn child. For smoking and excessive alcohol will harm a foetus who will actually be born. Someone who will later exist will actually suffer harm. But if the foetus is aborted, there is no later child who will be harmed. So we have two distinct questions: first, when does the foetus have interests and a right to life that should be protected like any other human being? And second, does it have an intrinsic value, whether or not it has a right to life?

To carry the argument further Dworkin suggests we need to make a number of other distinctions. First, between what has intrinsic value and what has instrumental value. Many things are valuable because they are of use to us in some way: cooking pots, oil, medicines and so on. These have instrumental value. But what is of intrinsic value is valued for its own sake, just because it is, whether or not it is of any use. We might say that a beautiful cloud formation, or one of Constable's sketches of clouds, are of worth of themselves, for themselves. We would want to acknowledge them even if there was no one around to view or admire them.

Second, there is a distinction between what is of incremental value and what is of intrinsic value. When something has incremental value the more we have of it the better. If there is a shortage of food, the more the better – at least until the shortage has ended. But when something has intrinsic value, it is not true that you necessarily want more. However sublime, there are probably enough Rembrandt self-portraits. A work of art is a unique accomplishment which we value for its own sake, without necessarily wanting more of the same.

On the basis of these two distinctions we can say that a human life is of intrinsic, not instrumental worth, and we do not necessarily want more and more of it. Indeed, if the world is in grave danger of over-population then it may be important that we do not have more and more lives. Their number may need to be limited.

Then there is the controversial fact that we value some things more than others. We value horses more than fleas, and this is not just because horses have been of use to us and fleas are a nuisance. We recognize that in horses there has been what we might term an evolutionary achievement. Evolution has developed a creature that brings forth our admiration; in the case of other creatures, such as tigers, it inspires our awe. Sometimes it is nature's achievement that we value, sometimes that of human beings. We value a minority language, say Gaelic, because it embodies and expresses what generations of human beings have put into it. If it died out it would be a real loss, not because we lack other languages with which to communicate, but because we recognize its value in itself. So also we might regret the dying out of a minority culture in the Amazon rainforest or the Kalahari desert. This highlights a good reason for being concerned about the future of the planet – not because we would violate the rights of unborn generations to come, but because life, and especially human life, is a miraculous, awesome coming about, the product both of nature and human culture.

This also brings out the fact that loss is not to be measured simply in terms of duration but of what has been put in both by nature and human beings. We feel the death of a three-year-old more than the loss of an infant and the loss of an adolescent more than that of a three-year-old. None of these losses are to be underestimated, they are all grievous. But in the case of an adolescent a huge amount has gone into his or her life. There are two terms from the field of economics that bring out the point, although I use them in a non-financial sense: *investment* and *value-added*. In a teenager there has been a huge investment of love and care, nurture and education. A teenager's life is already a significant achievement. There has been value added from the time of his or her birth. Similarly, most people feel – and the law reflects this – that a late abortion is a much more grievous loss than one in the very early stages of pregnancy. This is not just because at that stage we can see what is palpably going to be a live baby in a few weeks' time. It is because during the previous months the foetus has grown and developed into an extraordinary, complex and wondrous being. That development has taken place because the mother has put into the child not just nutrition but love and feeling, and it is now the object of great hopes and fears.

Dworkin makes a further distinction between what is put into this achievement by nature and what is put in by human care and culture. He then suggests that the real divide between conservatives and liberals on this issue is how they weigh the one against the other. Conservatives will weigh the contribution of nature above that which is contributed by the human environment, and vice versa.

Many aspects of Dworkin's argument can be accepted but it does depend on a clear assumption, one which was stated earlier, about when an entity gains rights. It is important to note that his is an assumption that not all will agree with. It is that such an entity cannot have interests and rights 'unless it has . . . some form of consciousness'.

A painting may not have interests, but animals do. They have an interest in staying alive, even though they may have no conscious awareness of this. Similarly a foetus has an interest in staying alive.

In talking about rights it is of course important to know how this word is being used. Dworkin has done great service elsewhere in his description of rights as 'trumps' which override all utilitarian calculations about what is for the best.[11] We have a right not to be tortured, even though it might be in the best interests of the state to gain information from us by that means. What is referred to here are basic human rights. But rights language in recent years has become extended far beyond this, for example with international conventions on economic and social rights. These cannot be absolute, overriding all other considerations, because their implementation depends on the state of development of the country under consideration. So rights language here is being used in the sense of a major moral claim which has to be taken into account and given very high, but not absolute, priority when in conflict with other rights.

On this basis, it is quite in order to talk about animal rights. This does not mean that animals have the rights of a human person. They have the rights of an animal. Beautiful foxes bask in the sun in my garden in the mornings. They have a right to live their life without being killed except for good reason. This right is not equivalent to the rights of humans, and there may be good reason to kill them, but it is still a right to be taken into consideration, a claim upon us.

Dworkin sharply distinguishes a rights-based opposition to abortion from a value-based one. But the distinction is not so sharp as he maintains. If I recognize something as having intrinsic value I am aware that it makes a claim upon me and that I have a responsibility towards it. This arises even in relation to inanimate objects like paintings which cannot be said to have interests, but which may have an intrinsic value that I recognize. Part of the act of recognition is that I am aware that I have a responsibility not to damage the painting either wilfully or inadvertently. This does not mean that the painting has rights. The rights belong to the owner of the painting who may then, from a legal point of view (not a moral one), do what he wants with it. Sometimes, as with a listed building, the rights of an owner are legally restricted, and this is because the wider community, whatever the owner might or might not think, regards the building as being of aesthetic or historic interest.

The situation is different with animals. We recognize that they have an intrinsic value as part of creation – part of God's creation, the believer will say. This value is to be acknowledged, affirmed and celebrated. Animals also have a life of their own, and therefore an interest in staying alive. From these facts it is clear that we have a responsibility towards animals. Corresponding to this animals have certain rights, although they must rely on other human beings to enforce those rights on their behalf. For example, a person can be prosecuted for cruelty to animals; a farmer who neglects his livestock can be taken to court by the RSPCA. Note that this does not apply to all animals: I can be prosecuted for torturing my cat but not for stepping on slugs on my path. The important difference here is obviously whether the animal is capable of feeling pain. Animals that feel pain have a certain degree of legal protection.

This protection is not absolute. Those of us who are not vegetarians allow animals to be killed so that we can eat them. Even more controversially, we allow animals to be used for research when this is necessary for the improvement of human health.

The body of international human rights law drawn up after the Second World War is one of the great achievements of that generation, but rights were not invented then. They are inherent in any legal system. Legal systems by their nature offer degrees of protection to different kinds of people. Even slaves in ancient Rome had certain protections. What we have seen in recent centuries is a widening out and equalizing of protections which in the past were only available to the elite – that is, men who, in the main, owned property. What the post-Second World War generation brought about was the conviction that certain rights are absolute, ones which override even reasons put forward by governments about what they judge to be in the best interest of the society (as outlined above in the example of torture). But most rights can find themselves in conflict with other rights, hence the need for courts to adjudicate between them. And this means that not all rights can be said to be absolute and overriding.

Legally enshrined human rights are grounded in a conviction about the moral worth and dignity of every human individual. But the reason this moral conviction takes on legal force, and needs to do so, is because in a deeply flawed world the value of the human individual is cruelly violated. In a perfect world (and in heaven) there would be no need to talk of rights. The worth of every person would be recognized, celebrated and acted on. But in the world as it is human beings need all the protection that the law affords.

Christopher Miles Coope offers a sustained critique of Dworkin[12] that is very clever and sophisticated, though marred by a tone that sometimes slips from irony into sarcasm, even bitterness. But this is an issue of life and death, and from his standpoint murder is being committed, murder that is supported by academics of high reputation like Dworkin, so that tone is perhaps understandable. The book is also marred by too many quotations from other authors and, because Coope clearly wishes to avoid being too obviously typecast, his main argument is not always as clear as it might be. But this is how I understand it.

Dworkin, as we have seen, believes that two kinds of argument are being used to oppose abortion. The second kind, the idea that the foetus has intrinsic value, is the one which Dworkin regards as having validity. Coope rightly points out that the words that Dworkin uses in relation to this position, such as 'sacred' and 'inviolable', do not seem to have much restraining effect on what he thinks is allowable. For despite this estimate of the intrinsic value of the foetus, Dworkin still allows the moral possibility of abortion in a wide range of cases, for example if the mother's career is going to be hindered by having a child. So the word sacred is not helpful in relation to this position, nor is inviolable, which implies an absolute prohibition on any hurt to the foetus under any circumstances. Intrinsic value is however an important and legitimate term to keep, if one believes it is applicable to the foetus. For something can have intrinsic value without that value overriding every other value.

Coope seems somewhat reluctant to pursue the idea of intrinsic value, on the grounds that it has no clear meaning. On the other hand, at the end of the book, he seems to affirm the idea very strongly. His main line of argument, however, is against Dworkin's view that the foetus has no interests, no good that has to be taken into account. According to Dworkin an organism only has interests when it is sentient, or perhaps even later, when it is capable of rudimentary consciousness. Coope points out first that it is important to distinguish between a person having interests, in the sense of choices and chosen goals, and having interests which belong to it as such even before consciousness. It is of course true that the foetus does not have chosen goals. However, it certainly has interests in the second sense, a good that needs to be taken into account. So do non-humans. We talk about the good of a species, or a particular dog or tree. A tree can be harmed. Certain things, like rain and water, help it to flourish. A foetus can certainly be harmed, by the mother taking drugs for example, while other things can work for its good. As indicated above, I agree with Coope at this point.

Second, this good belongs to the organism as such, by virtue of its nature, and is not dependent on its particular stage of growth. There are certain conditions that work for the good of an oak whether it is a sapling or an old tree. Similarly there are certain things that work for the good of the foetus by virtue of its nature as human. It is as human that it is helped to flourish or is hurt.

This leads on to the third point, that it is organisms that have interests, not inanimate objects. Pebbles have no interests. They cannot be helped or hindered in their development as pebbles. Puppies, however, can be helped in their development, and so can foetuses. Some things are in their interest and other things are not. Again, Coope is right to make this distinction.

Fourth, whereas Dworkin sees intrinsic value primarily in terms of what has been put into the entity, whether by nature or human effort, Coope thinks that loss of potential also needs to be taken into account. It may be true, as Dworkin suggests, that there is no consciousness in a foetus which can be said to lose out by loss of a future. But the foetus does have a good, a good which involves developing its full potential as a human being. Loss of this good is a real loss. That is true, but it is not in itself the deciding factor in how we weigh the loss of potential against the loss of an achieved good. I have suggested that we are right to give greater weight to achieved good.

Then, in the last part of his book, Coope criticizes the idea that interests and rights always go together and that the wrongness of murder is primarily a violation of someone else's right to life. He does not jettison the idea of a right to life but thinks that the main basis for the wrongness of murder is that there is a prior obligation to this effect. It is wrong even before any talk about a person having a right to life. Referring to Dworkin's view that society needs a taboo against torture, making it clear that in all circumstances it is wrong, and nothing can justify it, Coope suggests that this matches the language that needs to be used to denounce abortion: 'It hardly seems necessary to talk of rights. What is needed is a recognition of human dignity and worth, a taboo, a commitment, an everlasting No.'[13]

As this quotation makes clear, he seems to affirm the language of value, that is, of dignity and worth, having previously been uncertain about it. Certainly the position taken here is that this kind of language is central, and does have meaning.

What distinguishes the Roman Catholic position as maintained by Coope, together with those others who share it, is that the foetus in the womb has the absolute, overriding rights of a human person. That is why abortion is forbidden even to save the mother's life. The unborn baby's life is regarded as strictly equal to that of the mother.

Finding common ground

So where does this leave the argument over the moral status of the foetus for those who do not share the Roman Catholic view? The law does afford the foetus some legal protection. Abortion is still a crime unless it is carried out in accord with the Act. So we recognize that the foetus has some rights. Should those be absolute rights?

Two moral views are widely shared. First, most people believe that if there is a conflict between saving the mother's life and the life of the unborn child, it is the life of the mother that should be saved. As Dworkin rightly suggests, this widespread view, shared by great numbers of people who are opposed to abortion in almost all other circumstances, indicates that they think the foetus does not have the absolute right to life that we accord to a newborn baby.

Second, most people who support experiments on animals for the benefit of human health, however reluctantly and with all the proper qualifications, would say that it would be quite wrong to allow experiments on the foetus in the womb with a view to improving the health of babies in the future. Animals may, in certain carefully controlled conditions, be used for experiments, unborn babies may not.[14]

I am not for the moment arguing for the truth of either of these two moral convictions. I am trying to map out some common ground on which it might be possible to narrow the areas of disagreement over the moral status of the foetus. What the two moral convictions outlined above suggest is that although we think the status of the foetus does not have absolute value, it has more value than other members of the animal species. I am aware of course that this view will not be held by all – Peter Singer for example believes that the higher animals have the same rights as humans. But his is not a widespread view in our society.

So the question for those of us who do not share the Roman Catholic understanding of the early embryo on the one hand, or Peter Singer's view of animals on the other, is where do we draw the line? In the previous chapter I argued that the 14-day rule marked one clear boundary which is scientifically based and legally enforceable, and which can be ethically justified. At the other end, as it were, there is a clear boundary when the baby is viable. Although it is not totally certain where this boundary lies and the position may change in the future, there seem good medical reasons now for keeping it at the present 24 weeks. Another boundary would be when the growing foetus is able to feel pain. But a clear, scientifically based line for this has not yet been established. As discussed above, it seems to lie somewhere between 26 and 30 weeks.

One problem with all these discussions about the value of or rights of the foetus is that they tend to assume either the analogy with a separate, independent person, or with a body part. The truth, as earlier quotations from some women writers have shown, is that neither assumption quite works. My own position as it were builds inwards from two extremes.

First, rape. I find it intolerable that a woman who has been raped should be forced to bear the child that has been conceived as a result. It is possible that she might choose to do this and for the future child's sake not abandon it when she has a chance to do so. But that is different from forcing a woman who has conceived as a result of rape to bear the child. This is not to deny the intrinsic value of the foetus but to say that this value is outweighed by the wrong of inflicting further humiliation and pain on a woman whose whole being cries out in disgust against what has happened, and against the consequences. In this case I believe that the well-being of the mother takes priority. I also believe there are factors here to do with the well-being of the unborn child. We know that the relationship between a young baby and mother (or mother substitute) is crucial for the future holistic health of the child. It is of particular importance that the mother bonds with the child. Furthermore, there is already an incipient relationship between the child growing in the womb and the mother, a relationship which involves deep emotions, hopes and fears. If a child grows in the womb, and is then born to a mother who can feel only disgust and revulsion at it because of the circumstances of its conception, you cannot help wondering about how it will feel about itself, and therefore about the kind of life it will lead.

Second, at the opposite extreme, a woman decides to abort a foetus because it is a girl and she wants a boy. This, in the judgement of most people, is quite wrong not just because of the social effects of such an abortion on society as a whole (as seen in India), but because the reason is not a weighty one. A civilized society affirms that girl babies are of equal value to boys, and this inherent worth must be given priority over the woman's desire to have a boy.

Someone who thinks that abortion can be morally justified in the second instance, or conversely, thinks it ought to be forbidden in the first, does not fit into the kind of spectrum where I believe the debate lies. We either see that the first example is justified and the second not, or we do not, and if the latter is the case, a different kind of conversation has to be had altogether. What these two extreme examples show is that first, the foetus does not have such absolute value that allowing it to be born outweighs every other consideration. And second, that the mother does not have such absolute dominion over what is happening in her own body that she can do what she likes with what is there.

What the second example also brings out is that the intrinsic value of the foetus is something that society as a whole quite properly has an interest in. This is shown in a positive way through the provision of ante-natal care, and the concern doctors rightly have for the foetus in the womb. It is also shown in the laws on abortion which in theory only allow abortion in certain prescribed circumstances.

The position taken in this book is that after implantation in the womb and from about 14 days, the foetus has intrinsic value as a human individual with the potential to become a person and that its loss at any stage is to be regretted and may even be tragic. So, according to the 1983 resolution of the Church of England Synod, 'All human life, including life developing in the womb, is created by God in his own image and is, therefore, to be nurtured, supported and protected.'

The Church of England in its official resolutions has acknowledged that there are some circumstances when it might be right to have an abortion but only as limited exceptions to a basic opposition to it. As a briefing paper summarizing the position prepared by the Board for Social Responsibility put it, 'The Church of England combines strong opposition to abortion with a recognition that there can be – strictly limited – conditions under which it may be morally preferable to any available alternative.' This meant that, as the 1983 resolution stated, 'The number of abortions carried out since the passage of the Abortion Act 1967 is unacceptably high.'[15]

The number is still unacceptably high, as indicated by the figures quoted at the beginning of this chapter. None of the proposals that have been made in recent years to change the law in order to reduce the number of abortions has gained widespread support. It may be that the present law is about the best we can do in terms of balancing the various interests and claims involved in this issue. But other changes can and should be made. One advance in recent years has been the development of preimplantation genetic diagnosis, as described in the previous chapter. This means that for an increasing number of serious diseases parents who suspect that they might be carriers of the relevant genes can have their embryos tested so that only an embryo which is free of the condition is implanted. There is also preimplantation genetic screening, available for what is popularly known as Down's syndrome. These rapidly advancing medical techniques mean that women in the past who might have discovered they were carrying a child who would grow up with a very serious disease or a severe disability, and who would have thought of having an abortion as a result, need no longer find themselves in the position of deciding whether or not to make that choice.

Changes are important in other areas. What is needed first, of course, is much better teaching to young people about sex and the proper use of contraceptives. This should not just be about the mechanics of sex but about its seriousness – and in particular about its proper place in committed, long-term relationships.

Next, we also need a change in the moral climate of our society so that the claim of the unborn child in the womb to life is given proper priority in all the decisions that are made. In our society it is no longer the stigma it once was for a single person to have a child. Just the opposite. Women contemplating an abortion need to be given good counselling, and to be assured that if they decide not to have an abortion they will receive all the help they need both to give birth and either to support the child or to have it adopted.

3

THE END OF LIFE[1]

Christian medical ethics and end-of-life care[2]

In recent decades pressure has been building up to change the law to allow people to seek medical help in ending their own life. One reason for this, of course, is that we are all living so much longer. But closely related is the fact that medical technology now enables people to be kept alive with medical conditions from which in previous ages they would have died long before. The result is that many people seem to eke out their last days with a very poor quality of life, often to the distress of those who love them. Another reason for the pressure to change the law is the current emphasis on human autonomy and our alleged right to do what we want with our own lives. What Hamlet referred to as the ban on 'self-slaughter' has less moral force than it once did.

Some of the pressure for physician-assisted suicide is based on misconceptions or misunderstandings of what the Christian Church teaches about end-of-life care. First of all, therefore, it is important to set out certain basics of Christian medical ethics.

First, there is absolutely no obligation to prolong burdensome treatment when it is clear that it is doing no good. In other words, there is no need to prolong life at all costs. This has been the consistent teaching of both the Church of England and the Roman Catholic Church. It was famously expressed when a pope quoted (out of context) the nineteenth-century poet Arthur Clough:

> Thou shalt not kill:
> But need'st not strive,
> officiously to keep alive.

In recent years, however, some people have felt that there have been attempts in certain medical quarters to keep a relative alive at all costs. Anne Ridler wrote a poem, based on an earlier one by Robert Herrick, in which she referred to 'the artless doctor' who could do nothing more except let his patient die. Now, with so much effort going into keeping people alive, she prays:

> Grant me an artless doctor, Lord,
> Unapt with syringe, mask or knife,
> Who when my worn-out body's dead
> Will fail to bring me back to life.[3]

If people really are being kept alive at all costs, this is not good medical practice and it is contrary to Christian teaching. As Pope John Paul II's 1980 declaration on euthanasia put it:

It is also permissible to make do with the normal means that medicine can offer. Therefore one cannot impose on anyone the obligation to have recourse to a technique which is already in use but which carries a risk or is burdensome. Such a refusal is not the equivalent of suicide; on the contrary, it should be considered as an acceptance of a human condition, or a wish to avoid the application of a medical procedure disproportionate to the results which can be expected, or a desire not to impose excessive expense on the family or the community.

When inevitable death is imminent in spite of the means used, it is permitted in conscience to take the decision to refuse forms of treatment that would only secure a precarious and burdensome prolongation of life, so long as the normal care due to the sick person in similar cases is not interrupted. In such circumstances the doctor has no reason to reproach himself for failing to help the person in danger.

At this point there may be a contrast with some Jewish teaching. I remember hearing the late Lord Jakobovits, then Chief

Rabbi and something of an expert on Jewish medical ethics, say that from a Jewish point of view every last moment of life was precious in itself. The implication of this is that life should be prolonged as long as possible. That view is probably not now representative of the Jewish position, but as stated it is different from the Christian one, which says that if treatment is oppressive and is doing no good it is quite morally legitimate to request that it be stopped.

Second, there is a clear moral distinction between giving someone a painkilling drug which might have the effect of shortening life and giving that person a drug whose prime effect is to kill. Sometimes it is said that GPs are already killing thousands of old people. Now it may be true that a few are being deliberately killed. However, what is likely is that in the vast majority of cases the doctor, in order to control pain, has been giving the patient morphine or a similar drug whose side-effect might be to shorten life somewhat.

The reason this confusion arises is because some people, either inadvertently, or deliberately as a considered philosophical position, make no distinction between consequences which are intended and those which are foreseen but unintended, simply weighing all the consequences without making that distinction. In short, for them there is no moral distinction between life shortened as a result of morphine and life shortened as a result of cyanide. In both cases the consequence is the shortening of life.

For a Christian, however, actions can be intrinsically right or wrong – right or wrong in themselves even before any consequences are taken into account. Weighing consequences is an important part of making a decision, but it is not the only part. Linked to it is what is called the principle of double effect. This comes into play at a number of points in Christian moral theology. For example, an attack on a military target will result in a number of civilian casualties. Those casualties have to be taken into account when assessing the morality of the action.

It could be that the casualties are so extensive that they outweigh any possible gain that would be achieved by attacking the target. But it may be that it is essential to attack the target, and the civilian deaths incurred in doing so are not out of proportion to the importance of destroying the target. In this case the intention is to destroy the target. The civilian deaths are foreseen but unintended. They are unintended in two senses. They are unintended in that the attacker would much prefer that they did not happen, and he takes every possible step to minimize their number. They are also unintended in the immediate thrust of the action, for the rockets that are fired actually hit the military target, not the civilian houses around it.

It is important to note that there is a certain ambiguity about the word intention in this kind of discussion. For some people it refers to the mental attitude which is behind the action. So in an attack on a military target the mentality or motivation is to destroy the target while avoiding civilian casualties so far as is possible. But the word intention may also refer to the main thrust of the action. In this example the intention is disclosed by the fact that the rocket is directed at and hits the military target. As far as the moral discussion is concerned it is this latter meaning of intention which is the more important: the actual, immediate thrust of the action.

A fictional example occurs in the 2003 film based on Patrick O'Brian's novel *Master and Commander*. A ship caught in a terrible storm loses its mast. However, the mast is still attached to the ship by its rigging and this puts the whole ship in danger of being sunk. The captain orders the rigging to be cut so the mast can float free. Unfortunately there is a sailor clinging to the mast (he is in fact the best friend of the man ordered to cut the rigging) and he will almost certainly be drowned by this action. The sailor's death is foreseen but unintended. The intention of the action, cutting the rigging, is to save the ship. The action is judged proportionate because although one person drowns, all the rest are saved.

In a similar way, the intention of giving a patient a pain-relieving drug like morphine is to control the patient's pain. The fact that this also has the effect of reducing the person's life somewhat is foreseen but unintended. In this case the reduction of pain is regarded as a greater good than extending the life by a few days or weeks. The action is intrinsically right, in that it is directed towards reducing pain, and it is proportionate, in that the loss of a short period of life is a price worth paying for greater comfort at the end. This fact obviously chimes in with the first point above, about not being under an obligation to prolong life at all costs.

The distinction can be seen by examining what would happen if for some reason potassium chloride were administered in order to kill a patient but failed to do so. In order to carry out his intention the doctor would then have to administer more potassium chloride. If, however, morphine was injected and this, while controlling the pain, in no way shortened the person's life, the doctor would have succeeded in his intention. He would not administer more morphine in order to hasten death. His intention was to relieve pain and in that he had succeeded. As the Oxford philosopher John Lucas has written:

> Although we have to take account of such side-effects in deciding whether to take or not to take a course of action, if, contrary to our expectations, the side-effect does not come about, we do not take further action to make sure that it does, but on the contrary are glad that it has not . . . This shows that the side-effect is not what we want to happen, and so does not manifest our mind in the matter. There is no intention to kill in administering a painkiller, no disregard for the sanctity of human life.[4]

This distinction between what is intended and what is foreseen but unintended obviously depends, as indicated above, on a belief that certain actions are right or wrong in themselves even before considering the question of what effects they would have. The justification for this distinction is discussed later.

The third point about Christian medical ethics concerns the distinction between ordinary and extraordinary means of care, as already implied in the statement of Pope John Paul II quoted above. This is not relevant in every situation, but it is crucial to the consideration of some, such as cases where the patient is in what is known as a permanent vegetative state (PVS). There is a moral obligation in all circumstances to give a patient ordinary means of care, and this includes food, water and such comfort as is possible. But there is no obligation to give a patient extraordinary means of care if that care is burdensome or is apparently not doing any good. Of course, what was once considered an extraordinary form of care may, after being in use for some time, be regarded as routine, normal care. So the boundary is not always clear, particularly when it comes to nutrition and hydration being delivered by tubes into the stomach. But I will look at this issue in greater detail later, in relation to patients diagnosed as being in a permanent vegetative state.

For now, however, there are two further points to note by way of preliminaries that do not belong to moral theology, but bear upon the situation of end-of-life care. One is that it is now legal to draw up an advance directive or living will. This lays down in advance what you want to happen in the event that you are so ill in the future that you are unable to make a decision yourself at that time. Advance directives to refuse treatment are legally binding, although advance directives in relation to particular forms of treatment are not. For example, you might want to say that if towards the end of your life you are on a life-support machine, or in a deep irreversible coma, you do not wish to be kept alive. This is a way in which we can have an input into decisions about the end of our life which are entirely congruent with Christian moral theology. Such advance refusals of medical treatment now have legal force. In other words a doctor is legally obliged not merely to pay attention to them but to put them into effect.

The second point is that there have been huge advances in palliative care in the last 40 years. Dame Cicely Saunders pioneered this care at St Christopher's Hospice in south London. She worked on two basic principles. First, that with the proper, scientific administration of drugs, pain can in most cases be controlled. This means giving the right amount of drugs at regular intervals, not waiting until the pain starts. Second, that a supportive, caring environment should be created – one, in the case of St Christopher's, which is undergirded and suffused with prayer. She found that with these two elements in place almost no one expressed a desire for euthanasia. As a result of the model provided by St Christopher's, the hospice movement has taken off in most places in the UK, and palliative care has become a major medical specialism, so that even if people are not in a hospice, they can receive good-quality palliative care in hospital or at home.

This is not to say that things are yet perfect. Like other forms of medical care, the quality of palliative care can vary between various parts of the country, and according to the resources that are available. But it is an important factor in this debate that good palliative care is possible, and there is agreement that we need to continue both to improve it and make it universally available.

Voluntary euthanasia and assisted dying: the law

Over the last 50 years the pro-euthanasia lobby has become increasingly active and confident. In the last decade in the House of Lords, Lord Joffe introduced two bills to try and legalize assisted dying. Both were defeated, but there is no doubt that another attempt will be made before long, either there or in the House of Commons. In the summer of 2009 an amendment was proposed to the Coroners and Justice Bill in an effort to decriminalize the act of taking someone to the Dignitas clinic in Switzerland, where they can be given medical help to die. Again it was defeated, but a great deal of publicity ensued about people who had taken this course of action without in the end being prosecuted for it. Since then a legal case has resulted in a direction from the court to the Director of Public Prosecutions to draw up a set of criteria to make it clear under what circumstances a person may or may not be prosecuted for assisting another person to commit suicide, perhaps by helping him or her travel to the Dignitas clinic. In short, there is a gathering momentum. The pro-euthanasia lobby clearly feel that they are riding the tide of progressive history, and that one more wave will take them to a shore where people who are dying will be able to choose the time and place of their death. It is worth noting, however, that not all those usually regarded as liberal progressives are of one mind on this issue. Indeed, when Lord Joffe introduced his first bill into the Lords he said he was amazed to find I was opposing it because, as was probably true, we would line up together on almost every other liberal-progressive cause.

There is no doubt that some of the situations and stories of those who would like assistance in dying are heart-rending. But there are also extremely strong reasons for not passing a law which would make such assistance legal in principle. That said, I preface what I am about to write by emphasizing that if I found myself in a similar situation to some of the people we know or read about, I do not know how I would react, whether or not I too would want a physician to give me the means to die. So I do not approach the subject with any sense of moral superiority – or, I hope, with any lack of sympathy for people who find themselves in such an unbearable situation. I am also aware that many people feel it is not the issue of pain that is the main concern, but the sense of becoming increasingly undignified and dependent on others, as for example with those who have become almost totally helpless and perhaps doubly incontinent. The situation of such people is indeed often terrible and I have no idea at all how I would cope or react in similar circumstances.

Before we continue, it is important to be clear about the terminology that is used in debates about euthanasia. *Voluntary euthanasia* refers to situations when a patient asks that his or her life be ended, and a physician is present who administers the drugs that will kill that patient. *Non-voluntary euthanasia* occurs when a physician administers the drugs which kill the patient, but the patient has not been in a position to ask for this to be done because he or she has been in a coma or lacks the mental capacity to make a decision. *Assisted dying* refers to situations when a patient who is in the terminal stages of an illness requests and administers drugs which will kill him. The doctor prescribes the drugs but does not administer them and may or may not be present. *Assisted suicide* refers to situations when a patient who is not dying requests and administers drugs which will kill her.

There are two kinds of argument on the subject of euthanasia and assisted dying. One kind focuses on the law, on what it should allow, and what would be the overall effect of having a law which allowed assisted dying under certain conditions. The other kind focuses on the moral issue in itself. Understandably, most debate both within and outside Parliament has focused on the law and the implications of making such a law. This is the kind of argument in which believer and unbeliever alike will participate with what the philosopher John Rawls called 'public reasoning', a form of discussion in which there is a certain shared language and procedure. In other words, people do not appeal to their fundamental moral assumptions, whether or not they are religious. They consider, on the whole, the consequences of having or not having certain laws from the standpoint of a broadly shared understanding of the common good of society. I will consider first this argument about the effect of passing a law.

The effects of changing the law

The main arguments against allowing a law which would permit assisted dying, under some circumstances and with certain conditions, may be summed up as follows.

First, there is a possibility that the relatives of someone who is seriously ill will encourage that person to ask for euthanasia because they find the task of caring for him or her too onerous, or because they are in line to inherit from his or her estate and are worried that the money that would otherwise come to them is being used up in nursing home fees.

My own view is that this is very likely to happen in some cases, human nature being what it is, but that this in itself is not a strong enough argument against such a law if there were good grounds in favour of one. There is almost always a risk and a downside to everything we do, but the number of relatives wanting to treat a seriously ill person in this way would, in my view, be very limited, and legislation could be devised to ensure that the presence of financial considerations in a decision about assisted dying was a criminal offence.

Second, although the relatives of a seriously ill person might be exemplary in their care, the person herself might begin to feel a burden on them. She knows that she takes a great deal of looking after and that she is likely to deteriorate still further. She knows that her children, or carers, have many activities they would like to pursue, and that they are seriously tied up as a result of the care they are offering. She begins to feel it would be better all round if she asked for help in dying and stopped being such a burden on others. Perhaps she mentions this to her relatives, and the relatives assure her of their continuing love and support. Nevertheless, the ill person knows that in fact she is a burden to the others, notwithstanding their protests.

I take this argument very seriously. There is a real possibility that if there was a law allowing physician-assisted dying many old, frail, vulnerable people would feel themselves to be a burden and would begin to think that they ought to do the decent thing and ask for a doctor to speed them on their way.

The third reason against allowing such a law is that it would subtly change the relationship between patients and doctors. When someone sees a doctor at the moment there is an unequivocal trust that the doctor (despite whatever limitations he or she might have) will do his or her best to keep the patient healthy and alive. If there was a law allowing physician-assisted dying, there would be the seed of a doubt that the doctor was beginning to think, 'Is now perhaps the time when she might really ask for help in dying?'

It is very difficult to assess the strength of this argument, but some such change in doctor–patient relationships might take place if such a law were to be enacted.

The fourth reason is that if physician-assisted dying was available, this would detract from the continuing efforts that are needed to improve palliative care. Palliative care in the UK is among the best in the world, in strong contrast with a country such as Holland where voluntary euthanasia is available.[5]

Supporters of a bill for physician-assisted dying say that there is no reason why good palliative care should not coexist with the option of physician-assisted dying, and indeed that it should. This is of course right in theory. But in a world governed by scarce resources and where everything is a matter of priorities, there would be more than a danger, there would be a high likelihood that palliative care would suddenly begin to seem less important.

The fifth reason is the slippery-slope argument. As I have stated previously in this book, I believe we should be very cautious about appealing to this kind of argument, and indeed should be properly sceptical about its use. Nevertheless, such slopes do exist, and it is all too easy to find oneself on one. As we have seen, this is what happened with the 1967 Abortion Act, to take one example. The Act was supported by many good people, including leading Christians, who certainly did not have in mind that a situation would arise 40 years later when it seems possible to have an abortion almost on demand. It was certainly not the intention of the bill's original framers. However, because of major changes in the social climate over the last 40 years, what were originally thought of as tight conditions for an abortion are now interpreted very loosely indeed.

On the other hand, the slippery-slope argument is not always persuasive. In the first chapter of this book I concluded that, in relation to research on the early embryo, there is no likelihood of finding ourselves on a slippery slope. Although in theory there is a slippery slope between allowing research on early embryos and allowing research on the foetus, there are in fact very firm handrails which will stop our society getting on to that slope. So how persuasive is the argument about a slippery slope in the case of physician-assisted dying? Both Nigel Biggar[6] and Paul Badham[7] take the issue very seriously. Biggar devotes a major part of his book to a very careful consideration of the arguments, concluding that on balance he thinks such a slope does exist and there is a real danger of finding ourselves on it. Badham, who puts forward a specifically Christian case for assisted dying, nevertheless takes the example of what happened as a result of the 1967 Abortion Act very seriously indeed.

It is important to note that there are different kinds of slope. One is the kind of slope that was revealed on abortion. I shall call this slope one. The provisions of an Act originally conceived as permitting abortion under very carefully limiting conditions have in practice been widened out to include almost any abortion, at least up to three months. Similarly, legislation to allow assisted dying under very specific, tight conditions might be widened out to include assistance for people who are not dying but who are in deep distress, either as a result of their condition or more generally. The means might be self-administered or actually given by a doctor. The slope leads from assisted dying to assisted suicide or voluntary euthanasia for non-terminal conditions. The second slope – what I call slope two – is from assisted dying or voluntary euthanasia to non-voluntary euthanasia for non-terminal conditions. Voluntary euthanasia is initiated by the request of the patient. With non-voluntary euthanasia the patient may not be in a position to either give or withhold consent. The decision is made for the patient either by a doctor or a court. This raises further issues, for example the moral difference, if there is one, between biographical life and biological life, and I shall discuss these below. But the point here is that there could be a slope leading, for example, to relatives and a doctor agreeing that someone suffering from severe Alzheimer's is unable to make a decision himself, and should be given a painless death.

Slope one runs from assisted dying for the terminally ill to assisted suicide for people in distress as a result of their illness. That this slope exists cannot be denied. We have seen examples in recent years among those who have gone to Switzerland to die in the Dignitas clinic. There was the much publicized case of a young man, Daniel James, who had been so severely paralysed as a result of a rugby accident that he felt he could not go on living. Another much publicized case was that of Sir Edward and Lady Downes, a devoted couple who perished together in the clinic. Because Sir Edward had become increasingly deaf and blind and therefore dependent on his wife, who had been diagnosed with cancer, they decided to go to Switzerland together to die before their joint situation became any worse.

So there undoubtedly is such a slope, and many people are urging that we should slide down it on the grounds that we are quite entitled to decide the time of our death whatever state we are in. Indeed the founder of the Dignitas clinic believes just that. These slippery slopes will be considered in further detail later in this chapter.

Assisted dying in practice

Assisted dying or voluntary euthanasia is nevertheless now available in a number of places in the world: Oregon in the United States, the Netherlands, Belgium and Switzerland. In 2009 it also became available in the US state of Washington, and it is likely to be allowed soon in Luxembourg. It is important to look at what is happening in these other countries, for those who would like to see similar provision made in the UK believe that some of the arguments mentioned above can be shown to be groundless in the light of their experience.

The Netherlands has allowed voluntary euthanasia for some years. Assessing the situation there is complex, however, because the law against it remained in place until 2002; it was simply that physicians who carried out euthanasia under certain circumstances were not prosecuted. Assessing the evidence is also highly controversial. Some have argued strongly that there has been slippage to non-voluntary euthanasia, while others dispute this. For this reason, and because what is allowed in the Netherlands is euthanasia, rather than assisted dying, I will focus on Oregon, where assisted dying is legal.[8] Oregon, further-more, provided the model for Lord Joffe's bill in the House of Lords. I will also look at the evidence offered by the example of Oregon as interpreted by Paul Badham, who has written the strongest Christian case in favour of assisted dying. So, first, a word about Badham's argument as a whole.

Badham admits that behind his argument is the personal experience of the death of his father and other relatives, deaths which were prolonged, painful and very distressing. He also marshals evidence that the experience of people dying in hospices or at home with palliative care is not nearly so reassuringly peaceful as palliative care doctors claim, that many of those deaths are still very distressing. His argument is that Christians believe strongly that death is not the end, that they should welcome the opportunity to go into it lucid and pain free, knowing that 'underneath are the everlasting arms'. Suggesting that a moving farewell service with friends and relatives might be held before a lethal drug is taken, he argues that this should not be seen as an expression of despair or cowardice or rebellion, but as a natural way of behaving for those who believe in the God and Father of Jesus Christ, a God who does not want us to suffer unnecessarily. These more religious arguments will be considered in due course. But he also believes that the usual objections to changing the law can, in the light of the experience in the Netherlands and Oregon, be shown to be groundless.

Under Oregon's Death with Dignity Act (DWDA), terminally ill adults who fulfil the state's residency requirements can obtain and use prescriptions from their physicians for self-administered, lethal doses of medication. This Act has been in force since 1997, and the figures, which have to be published every year by the Oregon Public Health Division, are available for the years 1998–2008.

Since the law was passed, 401 patients have died under the terms of the law. The vast majority of these have been white and well-educated, and had been suffering from cancer. The most frequently mentioned end-of-life concerns were loss of autonomy, decreasing ability to participate in what made life enjoyable and loss of dignity.

During 2008, 88 prescriptions for lethal medication were written. Of these, 54 patients took the medication, 22 died of their underlying disease and 12 were alive at the end of 2008. In addition six patients with earlier prescriptions died from taking the medication, resulting in a total of 60 DWDA deaths during 2008. This corresponds to an estimated 19.4 DWDA deaths per 10,000 total deaths.[9] During 2008 the Oregon Medical Board found no violations of 'good faith compliance' and no physicians were sanctioned for 'unprofessional conduct' regarding the Act.

One of the major arguments against allowing assisted dying, as I mentioned above, is the fear that vulnerable old people, feeling that they were becoming an increasing burden, would feel they ought to request it. Badham argues that the experience of Oregon disproves this. As the quoted figures show, the people who have taken advantage of the Act are predominantly those who are used to taking control of their lives, who are educated and used to making decisions for themselves and others. They are not the obviously vulnerable. This is also borne out by an analysis of the age at which people take advantage of the Death with Dignity Act. Those aged 18–64 were over three times more likely to seek assistance with dying than the over-85 group. The average age of those dying in 2008 was 72, slightly older than the average for previous years of 69. Surveys by physicians and hospice professionals reveal that apart from those suffering from AIDS, who form a special sub-group, the vulnerable are not likely to seek assisted dying.[10] Those who seek help are predominantly those who are socially, educationally and professionally privileged.

The experience of Oregon seems also to disprove another major argument against legalizing assisted dying mentioned above; that is the fear that legalization of assisted dying would detract from good palliative care. The Oregon Hospice Association strongly opposed the DWDA when it was first proposed and fought a long drawn-out legal case against it. However, when they lost the case, eight years after the Act had come into force, they expressed relief because, to their surprise, demand for hospice places had actually risen during the period the Act had been in force.[11] The figures for 2008 show that the number of patients enrolled in hospice care was much greater than in previous years. This did not mean that these patients died in hospices, for 97 per cent died at home, but they were being cared for under the auspices of hospice palliative care. Over the eight years the percentage of people in Oregon who died in hospices rose from 22 per cent to 51 per cent, while the state also had the highest proportion of people who obtained their wish of dying in their own homes of any state in America.

The number of people who make full use of the DWDA is only small. According to Ann Jackson, the Executive Director and Chief Executive of the Oregon Hospice Association, 'Only 1 of 200 individuals who consider a request and 1 in 25 of these who formally make a request, will actually use a prescription.'[12]

Of those who obtain both the prescription and the lethal drugs, as the figures for 2008 quoted above show, not everyone goes through with it to the end. So the numbers are small, only 0.14 per cent of Oregonians actually choosing an assisted death. But it appears that the Act has offered many people reassurance.

So if we accept Badham's assessment of the evidence from Oregon, the main fears of those opposed to the Joffe bills in the Lords are unfounded. Oregon seems to have devised legislation for assisted dying which does not have the effect of burdening old, frail, vulnerable people, for those who take advantage of the law are predominantly from privileged groups.

Furthermore it does not undermine palliative care, for there has been an increase in the demand for it since assisted dying became legal. Nor in the period the Act has been in operation has there been slippage, either to allow for assistance in circumstances which are not terminal (slope one) or to any kind of non-voluntary euthanasia (slope two). That is not the end of the argument about slippery slopes, to which we must return in due course. But we can acknowledge that in relation to the experience of Oregon there is no evidence that legislation for assisted dying has harmful consequences of this kind. It is to be noted that there are some who do not accept this conclusion because there is no system in place in Oregon for properly reporting alleged abuses or for investigating whether in fact there have been any. Until such a system is in place, they argue, it is too early to draw sanguine conclusions from the experience of Oregon. However, the 2008 report of the Oregon Medical Board, quoted above, suggests that there is no evidence of any such abuses.

Religious opposition?

The supporters of a law permitting physician-assisted suicide sometimes claim that the opponents of such a law are merely religious conservatives who have always opposed progressive change in the past, who are doing so now and who always will in the future. Polly Toynbee in *The Guardian* is a notable example of this tendency.[13] As she has written, 'It was a cabal of bishops, rabbis and assorted religious enthusiasts who wrecked the Joffe bill in the Lords.'[14]

In fact, however, in the Lords the opposition to Lord Joffe's two bills on assisted suicide was led by a palliative care doctor, supported by all the other medical practitioners in the House. Furthermore there is not a single palliative care doctor in the UK who supports such a bill. It is surely remarkable that the people most in touch with the terminally ill should be so opposed to the introduction of such a bill. Polly Toynbee admits that palliative care doctors and nurses can be wonderful, and she saw this in action with her own mother. She also admits that palliative care is a branch of medicine 'exceptionally heavily dominated by the deeply religious who believe only God disposes'.

The last part of that sentence may or may not be true, but it is true that this exceptional care more often than not comes from people with a profound religious conviction which leads them to work for the alleviation of suffering and the human support of those in distress. Toynbee describes the influence in the debate of these skilled, caring people as 'immense – and baleful'. Yet these are the people who have, hour by hour, day by day, close contact with people who are dying. These are the people who are doing all they can to make the dying comfortable physically, emotionally and spiritually. Are not these just the kind of people, and this the kind of experience, which in any other field would be regarded as of overriding significance?

That said, there is a grain of truth in what Polly Toynbee and others like her believe. Earlier I mentioned that the issue of whether the law should be changed or not was discussed in the House of Lords, and is mostly discussed elsewhere, in terms of public reasoning, a form of argument in which no particular religious or secular standpoint is claimed for the reasons adduced, these reasons being available for agreement or disagreement by believer and non-believer alike, using the same kind of arguments. However, the concept of public reasoning is not quite so neutral as some believe. It is probably true that though the argument ostensibly takes place on the same ground, the weight given to different kinds of reasons is affected by a person's basic stance on life. For example, as we shall see below, the whole question of dependence and dignity is understood differently from a Christian perspective. So also is the question of the redemptive possibilities that come with suffering.

The slippery-slope argument outlined above also depends heavily on whether one takes an optimistic or a pessimistic view of human nature. If you take the dark side of human nature seriously, then you will also take seriously the possibility that people will exploit situations in a harmful way. The Christian Church has always taken the view that in legislation we have to take this dark side into account. As Reinhold Niebuhr put it, we are not only made in the image of Christ, we are crucifiers of Christ. So in the debates about the effects of changing the law it is probably true that people's basic understanding of what it is to be a human being affects how they understand and weigh up the different rational considerations. It is not that religious people in the Lords appealed to what God did or did not want. They did not do that in this debate. But they did bring to bear upon the rational argument certain assumptions and presuppositions which would not have been shared by secular supporters of such a bill.

The ethics of assisted dying

There is not of course a total divide between the law and morality. On the contrary, all the considerations I have discussed in relation to changing the law bear upon morality as well. However, in addition to those consequential arguments which form part of moral decision-making, there is the question of the morality of an act in itself. For example, it is possible for someone to say that a country ought to have a law which allows abortion under certain clearly defined circumstances, because the alternative would be worse for society as a whole, while personally taking the view that abortion is always wrong and she would never have one herself or advise anyone else to do so. Some Roman Catholics adopt this position, even though the Roman Catholic Church in its official teaching takes a much stronger line: namely that abortion being wrong in itself, it is always wrong for a society to allow for it, even in the most exceptional circumstances. This is an issue on which, from an official Catholic point of view, it is not possible for a person to have one standard while at the same time allowing society in its laws greater latitude. So I shall now consider the morality of assisted dying in itself, whatever position one takes on the possibility of allowing for it in law. For it could be that, like abortion, one might regard it as wrong in principle, as an act which one could never countenance for oneself, while at the same time thinking that a society ought to allow for it.

A Christian approaching the subject in this way might begin with two arguments that do not command widespread support today. One is that it is God, not we ourselves, who should decide when we die. It is God who disposes, as Polly Toynbee put it. All things are in his good hands and under his providential care, and our role is simply to trust and let nature take its course. The trouble with this argument is that because we believe God has now given us responsibility in so many spheres of life, it is difficult to draw the line at the point where we die. For example, we now take control, so far as we can, over the number of children born to us and the time at which we have them. We take steps to safeguard their future health in so far as it is in our power to do so. God has given us the responsibility of using our brains and skills, in cooperation with natural forces, for human well-being. So why should we stop there? What is wrong with also taking responsibility for the time and manner of our death? In his famous *Letters and Papers from Prison*, written during the Second World War, Dietrich Bonhoeffer castigated those religious apologists who rooted their theology in our areas of weakness and uncertainty. He called us to a new Christian maturity.

The Stoics of old regarded suicide at the right time as an honourable and noble way of dying. Some people regard the joint suicides of Sir Edward and Lady Downes in a similar way: a perfectly appropriate taking of responsibility, an act of courage, at a rationally decided point in their lives, before a final distressing end. So I am not going to appeal (at least in a direct way, though I intend to return to it in a more nuanced way later when I consider the balance between making things happen and letting them happen) to the argument that God decides the moment when we should die – even though Polly Toynbee and other atheists too often assume that this is the basis of the Christian opposition to assisted dying. I believe the considerations that a Christian brings to the argument are more subtle than that, and they derive from both ethics and theology.

That said, however, it is also important to point out that respect for people's freedom of choice cannot be the only con- sideration in this or in any other debate. The reason is simple.

If we greatly value our human capacity to choose, and we think that other people's choices should always be taken into account, this must be on the basis of a wider framework of values. Otherwise why should we value choice as such? If nothing else has value then there are no grounds for thinking that the act of choice alone is of worth. So if we believe that our capacity to make free, rational choices is greatly to be valued, this carries with it the consequence that there is a wider framework of values and that there are other claims upon us as well as that of taking into account people's choices. If we are rejecting the idea that it is God and God alone who should decide when we die, we equally have to reject the notion that it is simply a matter of individual choice without reference to other moral considerations.

In the foregoing discussion on the law and the effect of changing it to allow for assisted dying, I stressed that the argument was couched in terms of the consequences of doing so. But I also mentioned that some people think that certain actions are right or wrong in themselves, even before we begin to weigh up the consequences. One reason we might take this point of view in relation to assisted dying is because, as mentioned above, it is God, not we ourselves, who should decide when we die. However, there are various other grounds for thinking that some things might be right or wrong. One is that we simply see something to be the case. A child is being treated cruelly. Why is it wrong? It just is. There is no better justification, it is said, than just seeing that this is so. My own view is that all the famous ethical theories, when you think them through as far as they will go, depend in the end on a simple act of recognition: a recognition that something has value. Reasoning is important, but there comes a point where reasoning can take us no further and we are in the business of moral discernment – cruelty is wrong, kindness is right.[15]

Another reason for thinking about right and wrong in ways other than merely assessing the consequences of particular

101

actions, is the indispensability of clear, universal rules if human societies are to exist at all. The justification for such rules lies in the consequences that would follow if the rules themselves were widely ignored. Take for example the injunction against stealing. In order to make any kind of life we must have some kind of security that our possessions will remain ours so long as we want them. I am not referring to inordinate riches, but to basic things like somewhere to live, the ability to make a home that is moderately comfortable, and so on. Where there is total anarchy and such assurance is absent, life as we know it ceases to exist. So we have a clear, firm moral commandment, which takes effect in the law of all countries, that stealing is morally wrong and a crime. The justification for this law lies in the consequences of not having such a law, or not enforcing it. In other words, it is not the consequences of an individual act that are taken into account but the consequences of having or not having a particular moral rule and law.

Most of the Ten Commandments – some would say all of them – can be justified along these lines. From a theological point of view, it might be said that these are the ethical rules and laws devised by God for the existence and maintenance of human community. God, being all good and all wise, knows wherein our happiness lies and therefore has given us this basic blueprint for human living. He knows that keeping these laws will enable humans to live together in harmony. In fact the necessity of these laws, or most of them, can be easily discerned by anyone who thinks about the issue, whether or not that person has a religious faith. When I was a curate I used to take regular RE classes in our local Church of England primary school. One day I asked the class of eight- and nine-year-olds to imagine they were living with others on a desert island and had been given the task of coming up with some basic rules that would enable them to live together without squabbling. It was interesting how close each answer came to one of the Ten Commandments.

So there are certain moral rules, expressed in law, which are absolutely fundamental for human community. There can be no human society without them. Are these rules absolute? Or, in terms of the present discussion, given that it is wrong to kill other people or help them kill themselves, are they to be observed at all times, in all places and under all circumstances? The short answer is: 'No, there might be exceptions.' I should stress that I am not talking about killing by the police or the army, where all kinds of other considerations need to be brought into the discussion, nor am I talking about the shortening of life that may come about as a side-effect of the use of painkilling drugs, which was discussed in connection with the principle of double effect. I am talking about the direct killing of people who pose no threat or harm – traditionally called the innocent.[16]

There is the well-known example of a lorry driver who becomes trapped in the cab of his burning oil tanker. He is shortly to be engulfed in flames, but you are at the window of the cab and have a revolver in your hand, which he begs you to use. The moral course of action at that point is to shoot him. The reason is that his death is absolutely certain, immediate and horrible. The most loving course of action is to save him from the worst agony.

It is interesting that the very distinguished group of philosophers, theologians, doctors and lawyers that produced *On Dying Well* admitted that there could be extreme situations when it would be morally right to kill someone or ask to be killed oneself: 'as might happen, for example, in the jungle, in emergencies and accidents or in war, where medical aid is lacking or insufficient, exceptional cases could conceivably arise in which deliberate killing would be morally justified as being in the best interest of the person concerned'.[17]

Karl Barth's view on suicide is also interesting, because again it allows for exceptions. He thought suicide could be legitimate if done out of love for God or others, for what he called a definite service. He then went on to talk about when suicide would not be justified, and this will be discussed later. But the point here is that he did not think the injunction against suicide was absolute.

One theological reason why no one moral norm is an absolute is that this would place the moral rule in an equivalent position to God himself. Only God is absolute. In this life we sometimes find ourselves in a situation whereby we have to make an act of discernment between different kinds of goods and different moral norms. God is not to be identified with any one of these. An exception might be made in respect of the injunction to love, for God is love. But as will be shown in a moment, when we actually try to work out what this might mean in a particular situation, it will often mean opening up all the old debates; we find ourselves in the position of having to choose between different goods and different norms, none of which is able to claim absolute priority in every situation.

The position on moral rules and laws taken here is one which I would describe as *universal but not exceptionless*. This is a perfectly orthodox position and one taken, for example, by Thomas Aquinas in relation to stealing. The prohibition against stealing is a universal moral norm. It applies in all societies at all times. However, Aquinas argued that if a man and his family were starving and the only way to survive was to steal, stealing in those circumstances could be seen as a justified exception.

Two general points need to be made about this argument to avoid misunderstanding. First, it is obvious that exceptions by their very nature must be exceptional. They occur in borderline situations and they are likely to be very few indeed. Clearly, if there were a large number of exceptions the moral force of the rule would be undermined.

Second, the position taken at this point considers the consequences of having or not having certain rules, in particular the law that forbids euthanasia. This *rule utilitarianism* is to be distinguished from what is known as *act utilitarianism*. On the basis of the latter philosophy you take into account the consequences of a single act. In terms of the present debate, an act utilitarian position would be that taken by a person who simply considered the immediate effect on those he knew of seeking to end his own life. He would not consider the effect of having or not having the law in the first place. Or you might weigh up the consequences of lying or not lying in a particular situation and decide that your lie is not actually going to have a very detrimental effect. But, on the basis of the position taken here, the moral norm against lying is a highly significant factor in itself. A person in a tight position where he feels there is a strong, morally based reason to tell a lie has to take into account that the injunction to tell the truth is a crucial moral claim totally independent of whether that particular lie is going to have serious consequences or not. For example, when in the 1960s Prime Minister Harold Wilson famously denied that the pound was going to be devalued, although he knew that the next day that very thing would indeed happen, from a moral point of view he could not just weigh up the consequences of that one particular lie. He had to take into account the fundamental importance of truth-telling for society as whole.

Those who argue in favour of assisted dying are not for the most part suggesting that the law forbidding people to help others commit suicide should be rescinded. What they are suggesting is that there are exceptional situations where it would be right to go against the universal norm, and that it would be possible to allow for these exceptional cases by careful legislation along the lines of that which now exists in the state of Oregon. Those who oppose a change in the law ask first whether these cases really are so exceptional that they justify breaking a universal moral norm, and second whether, if they were encompassed in legislation, the effect would not be, little by little, to undermine the moral norm.

Mutuality and interdependence as fundamental to personhood

As indicated in the figures from Oregon quoted on page 94, a powerful reason why many are drawn towards physician-assisted suicide is not the fear of pain as such, but the fear of loss of dignity and increasing dependence on others, experienced for example by many people with severe neurological disorders. This is very real and understandable. However, the Christian understanding of what it means to be a human being brings further considerations to bear.

First, dependence is a feature of life from the moment we are born. The idea of human beings as isolated individuals, taking lonely responsibility for their lives, is one that has grown up since the Enlightenment and flies in the face of both human experience and Christian theology. The fact is that we human beings are dependent on one another as part of our very humanity. To repeat Austin Farrer's words, already cited in the first chapter, mind is a social reality. There is no such person as a totally isolated or self-sufficient human being. This reality is a reflection of ultimate reality, the life of the blessed Godhead as Father, Son and Holy Spirit. This reality is of course beyond anything we can conceive or convey in words, but what it suggests is that the social nature of human beings is a pale reflection of the perfect mutual interdependence of the persons within the Godhead. A person is always a person-in-relationship, what Africans call *Ubuntu*. This relationship dimension is not an optional add-on. It is integral to what it is to be a human being. It is, from a Christian point of view, a human being made in the image of God, who is in himself persons-in-relationship in a life of perfect mutual dependence and indwelling.

We all like to feel in control of our lives, to be independent and not beholden to others. But a truer understanding of what it is to be a human being admits the possibility of being dependent – and therefore vulnerable. We resist this. But perhaps in doing so we are resisting the truth about ourselves.

Then again, the Christian faith has something to say about the dignity and worth of human beings. This does not reside in our ability to control the direction of our lives. It belongs to us simply as human beings. Of course one of the marks of this uniqueness as creatures made in the divine image is that we can think and choose, love and pray. We can take responsibility for our lives and to some extent control them. But in whatever distress a person finds herself, perhaps through not being able to take full control of her life, she has not lost her essential worth and dignity as a human being, and there will be some vestige remaining of her capacity to think and choose, love and pray. Few would deny that it might feel very undignified to be totally dependent on others for all the functions of daily living. Again, I do not know how I would feel, cope or react if I was in that position. But this does not take away from the fundamental truth that our dignity as human beings does not reside in our ability to control our lives. The idea that it does is again a result of a distortion that has entered the Western mentality since the seventeenth century.

People who argue in favour of assisted dying say that to offer this to people in dire distress is the compassionate thing to do. Indeed those who oppose the legislation are sometimes accused of failing in compassion. A person with a debilitating neurological disorder pleads to be put out of his misery. He is in great distress of mind, and as he looks ahead he knows that things can only get worse. He pleads with you. He may even point out that we are prepared to put our pets out of their misery by taking them to the vet to be put to sleep for ever, so why should he be treated worse than the family dog? As Paul Badham puts it, in words quoted by Lord Joffe in the foreword to Badham's book:

When people's sufferings are so great that they make repeated requests to die, it seems a denial of that loving compassion which is supposed to be the hallmark of Christianity to refuse to allow their requests to be granted. If we truly love our neighbours as ourselves, how can we deny them the death we would wish for ourselves in such a condition?

No one will be unmoved by such a plea. Clearly the children of Sir Edward and Lady Downes were so moved, for they agreed to take their parents to Switzerland so they could be put out of their misery. In another case, when a woman doctor was taken to Dignitas, her son was initially very reluctant to agree to her request but eventually saw that it was right and agreed to accompany her.

The implication of Badham's words is that not acceding to the request of people in such a situation is a failure of compassion. Indeed I once received a bitter letter from a man whose wife was very ill and who eventually took her to Switzerland to die, accusing me of just this lack of compassion because of my stance opposing assisted dying, and who added that because of this he had decided to leave the ministry of the Church.

But the compassionate course of action does not always mean giving people what they want. We know, for example, that it is clearly not right in every case to accede to a person's request for help in committing suicide. If a depressed teenager asks for help in this way, the moral course of action is to refuse to do what she asks and to find some other way of helping her, perhaps trying to get medical help for her depression. Acceding to a person's request is not always the compassionate thing to do. Sometimes the compassionate course of action is to refuse it. For as the philosopher Basil Mitchell pointed out a long time ago, to love someone is to have in the forefront of our mind that person's well-being and the question of how we can contribute to it. *It does not answer the question.* To answer the question about what is the most loving or compassionate course of action is to reopen all the old questions of philosophy and theology. So we cannot assume that to agree to help a person kill himself is always the most loving thing to do.

For example, we might think that letting that person kill himself might be the most compassionate action in relation to him, but that legislating to allow for it might be a social evil because of the ill-effects discussed earlier. In that case you would have to make an act of judgement and choose between compassion for the individual concerned and lack of compassion for society as a whole. You might judge that the common good, the good of society as a whole, outweighed the compassion that was due to this particular individual in these particular circumstances.

There is also the question of whether it really would be the most compassionate course of action, even in relation to the individual. For a further consideration rises from the message that might inadvertently be sent if we did so agree. In agreeing to allow a person in her distress to kill herself with the help of a doctor, would we in fact be sending a subliminal message to her that we no longer really want her with us, that she is becoming too much of a burden for us? After all, a prime expression of the love we feel for someone is that we actually want that person with us. We do not want to send her away. We value having her with us. We want her.

In response that person might say, 'I much appreciate you saying that and I believe it, but my life is intolerable and I would still rather die now.' Again, it could be pointed out that to allow our natural desire to keep someone we love with us to override the desperate and reiterated request of the person that she be allowed to die is just selfishness. She wants to go, and however much you want her to be with you, if you love her you should let her do what she says she wants – and perhaps goes on insisting she wants, despite your repeated protests and pleas.

So this aspect of the argument is not one that can be easily settled. All that can be said is that just because a person has asked you to help her die it cannot automatically be assumed that the most loving thing to do is to agree to her request. It could be that a continuing reaffirmation of your love and care for her would make her feel that – despite every-thing – it was still worthwhile continuing in this life for the time being.

Suffering

In the past people believed that human suffering was directly willed by God for some purpose. Either it was a punishment for sin, or it was designed to test us or to further our moral and spiritual growth. The continuing resonance of the book of Job lies in the fact that Job refused to accept this conventional religious wisdom.

The fact is that physical pain is part of the physical world and plays a crucial part in evolution and our continuing survival. It is nature's warning mechanism. A child comes too near a fire and feels pain. The child backs away. Without this warning light we would not stay alive for very long. When a part of the body hurts, it is a sign that something is wrong and needs attending to.

The starting point for thinking about the relationship between God and his creation today must be the genuine autonomy which God has given the universe, an autonomy that comes into conscious freedom with us human beings. There is nothing anti-religious about such a view. It is simply to take seriously what it means to be created. To be created is to have a life of one's own, whether as an atom or a star, an insect or a human being. When God says 'Let there be . . .' he really does let things be. If this is the case, it is very difficult at the same time to affirm that everything that happens is willed by God. It is true in one sense of course, in that God has willed creation into existence and wills it to have a genuine life of its own. But it is not true that every individual event that happens is willed by him. A great deal is clearly contrary to his will.

This does not mean that God simply sets the universe going and stands back to observe what happens. Christians believe that God is involved with his universe at every point, in particular by drawing human beings into a relationship with himself, so that they can share in his great purpose. Christians further believe, of course, that God has gone to the limit with this involvement, coming among us in Christ and sharing our human anguish to the full. Now, risen, ascended and glorified, he continues this work through the power of the Holy Spirit, in union with his followers.

On the basis of this view we have to say that pain is part of the cost of being alive at all, and in that sense God wills it. But it is not true that God wills all particular pains. Indeed the opposite is the case. When pain no longer fulfils its primary function of warning us, or when nothing can be done to stop it, it is contrary to the will of God. Indeed the whole of Western medicine, which owes so much to Christianity, is based on the conviction that health is God's prime will for us. So, rightly, we do all we can in the final stages of a person's life to keep him or her out of pain.

Now it is certainly true that Christians both in the past and very often today have tried to see pain in a more positive spiritual light than I have so far suggested. In a famous statement by Paul he rejoices in his own suffering because it means that he can help to complete 'what still remains for Christ to suffer in my own person' (Colossians 1.24, REB). This need not – and should not – be taken to mean that our human suffering has any role in relation to God's attitude to us, which is one of welcome and in-gathering. But redemption ultimately means bringing the whole of humanity into a new kind of relationship with God and one another. For this purpose the work of Christ continues through his disciples in the power of the Holy Spirit. It may very well be that, like St Paul, a Christian will believe that his or her suffering, however caused, can be offered to God for his purpose. It may also be that the person who so offers his or her suffering is seen by others to have developed remarkable qualities of spiritual strength and serenity. However, two vital points need to be made in relation to this.

First, it is contrary to what we mean by the word love to think that God designs painful situations for individuals in order that they can develop moral and spiritual qualities. We would not think much of a friend who tripped us up on the stairs and broke our leg with a view to us developing qualities of patience and sympathy for others in a similar position. Friends do not act like that, and nor does the Christ who calls us his friends (John 15.11–17).

What we have to face is the fact that the physical pain of life is a condition of being here at all. Furthermore, the general toughness of life means, in the famous phrase of John Keats, that we experience it as a 'vale of soul-making'. As Edwin Muir put it in his wonderful poem:

> But famished field and blackened tree
> Bear flowers in Eden never known.
> Blossoms of grief and charity
> Bloom in these darkened fields alone.
> What had Eden ever to say
> Of hope and faith and pity and love
> Until was buried all its day
> And memory found its treasure trove?
> Strange blessings never in Paradise
> Fall from these beclouded skies.[18]

Second, following on from this, if it is true that Christians believe God is ceaselessly at work seeking to draw some unique good from every situation, however dire, then individual Christians will be engaged in a similar struggle to find whatever good might be extracted in their own circumstances. But this struggle is a vocation, something they feel is a key part of their relationship with God at that time. It is not a policy that can be imposed on others, nor can it be laid down as a general rule for all people irrespective of their religious faith. In fact, we sometimes find in experience that what Muir referred to as 'strange blessings . . . in . . . these beclouded skies', the hope and faith and pity and love that were not part of the Eden experience, are exhibited by a whole range of people, not just Christians. Many people, without faith as well as with faith, show extraordinary courage and concern for others as they are dying.

So a Christian approaching the end will seek to use this situation as an opportunity for widening his or her sympathy for others in a similar or worse situation, holding them up in prayer, and for an increased sensitivity and concern for those around. Such a Christian would hope at the end to be able increasingly to let go into God, as Jesus is reported by Luke as doing on the cross, with the prayer 'Father, into thy hands I commend my spirit.' But suppose the situation becomes impossible and the situation totally unbearable? God is not a sadist. He does not want us to continue in pointless suffering. Would it be right at that point to ask for a lethal dose?

Speaking personally, I would emphasize again what I said at the beginning of this chapter, namely that I do not know how I would react in such a situation. I am conscious of the words of Jesus to his disciples in the Garden of Gethsemane: 'Pray that you may be spared the test.' This is echoed in the Lord's Prayer when we pray 'Do not put us to the test' (REB) or 'Do not bring us to the time of trial' (NRSV). For although most modern versions of the prayers used in the liturgy have settled for the old word, temptation, as being more familiar to people, in fact the Greek word that Jesus used in the Garden of Gethsemane, and which appears in the Lord's Prayer, is *peirasmos*, which refers to the final testing of character that reveals what we are really made of.[19] It is not cowardice to pray this prayer, just a sober realization that as human beings we are frail, and we cannot in any way guarantee that we will act courageously when the time comes.

If we did finally decide it was too much, and that no conceivable good could be achieved by going on, would it be wrong to ask for a lethal dose? Immanuel Kant said, 'A suicide opposes the purposes of his Creator; he arrives in the other world as one who has deserted his post; he must be looked on as a rebel against God . . . Human beings are sentinels on earth and may not leave their posts until relieved.'[20]

Paul Badham argues against Kant that someone seeking assistance in dying should not be regarded in any of these ways, and I have already said I am not relying on the argument that only God should decide the moment when we depart this life. We have to take our human responsibility in every aspect of life, including dying, seriously. We can and should make responsible choices. But there is a more oblique way of approaching this, and that is through our understanding of natural processes. It is of the essence of modern humanity that we interact with and shape natural processes for human well-being. It is natural for us to use our God-given minds and skill in this way. However, as I pointed out in the first chapter, we have learned over the last 50 years that certain kinds of intervention in nature, which were thought to be wholly good, have turned out to have destructive consequences. In the 1960s it was discovered, for example, that the widespread use of pesticides, while undoubtedly increasing food production, was having a destructive effect on many other areas of nature: butterflies, birds, the quality of water and so on. We began to think much more holistically in terms of ecosystems and the balance in nature. Or to take another example, China's drastic policy of permitting only one child per family, with huge numbers of abortions as a result, has resulted in a situation in which there will not be enough young people at work to support a rapidly increasing older population. So the one child per family policy is being reversed. This is not of course an argument against having national policies. We certainly need them now in relation to such issues as climate change and the future challenges of refugees and shortages of food and water. It is simply to suggest that taking a decisive, interventionist step – as for example allowing people to decide the time they die – is at least worth questioning. Is this one of those areas where, on the whole, it is simply best to let nature follow its course rather than taking the violent step of suicide, while human skill does all it can to control pain, and human care does all it can to give the person a sense of dignity and worth right to the end?

Letting nature take its course was seen by Pierre Teilhard de Chardin in two stages. In the first stage of life the self develops and grows, while in the second stage, what he termed 'the forces of diminishment' had a role to play in further growth. In one of his prayers he wrote:

When the signs of age begin to mark my body (and still more when they touch my mind); when the ill which is to diminish me or carry me off strikes from within or is born within me; when the painful moment comes in which I suddenly awaken to the fact that I am ill or growing old; and above all at that last moment when I feel I am losing hold of myself and am absolutely passive within the hands of the great unknown forces that have formed me; in all those dark moments, O God, grant that I may understand that it is you (provided only my faith is strong enough) who are painfully parting the fibres of my being in order to penetrate to the very marrow of my substance and bear me away within yourself.[21]

Teilhard de Chardin puts in the qualification 'provided only my faith is strong enough'. Does that mean that if one asks for a lethal dose it is a sign of lack of faith, a failure of hope, an act of despair?

We might add to this the words of St Paul:

God keeps faith and will not let you be tested beyond your powers, but when the test comes he will at the same time provide a way out and so enable you to endure.

(1 Corinthians 10.13, REB)

Those who argue for a Christian basis for assisted dying would point out that, contra Paul, people are tested beyond their powers. They can be broken by suffering. They can lose their faith as a result of it, sometimes in the course of a distressing death. They would say that in those circumstances asking to depart this life is not necessarily a failure of faith and hope. It is not desertion of our post. For if a person makes a responsible decision about the end of his or her life, perhaps with a farewell service involving family and friends before taking a lethal dose, that person is going into death with a firm trust in God and his goodness, with hope of everlasting life.

Against that attractive picture, however, it must be asked whether a Christian can ever say that there is a situation in this life where it is no longer possible to make an act of self-transcendence towards God and other people, no longer possible to appreciate and value what is around us, no longer possible to offer some kind of prayer, where it is no longer possible for God to draw some unique good out of the present distress. We may feel that is the case – but from the standpoint of Christian faith that feeling cannot be taken as a final theological truth. The theological truth is that God is present in every situation, and where we are open to God, there will be God's blessing, no doubt mostly unknown to us.

There is a remarkable witness to this in the life of Jean-Dominique Bauby, a magazine editor who suffered a major

116

stroke and was in a coma for three weeks. When he woke up he was totally paralysed, speechless and able to move only his left eyelid. During the 15 months he spent in this situation before his death he dictated a book about his experience by signalling with his eyelid. What he conveyed in an utterly moving way was the joy of seeing his children and the way they continued to express their love for him.[22]

Karl Barth has written that there could be a morally justified suicide out of love for God or others, for what he called a definite service, but he went on to write:

> But such suicide would never be motivated . . . by despair about the worth of one's life or of one's failure to make oneself significant, or by wilful assertion of control . . . desperate suicide would be the result of mistakenly supposing that estimating the worth of our lives, or endowing them with significance, is something that we are capable of doing; suicide as an assertion of mastery is but a futile and hubristic rebellion against our creaturely limitations.

I do not myself think that the words 'hubristic' and 'rebellion' are justified, for reasons adduced earlier about the human responsibility that has been delegated to us by God. However, what Barth writes in the first part of the paragraph reinforces the view I have expressed that there is no point in our lives when we can say, from a Christian point of view, that our lives are useless, or that going on living has no significance.

There is another aspect of this, though, and that is the issue of gratitude. Christians agree that life is a gift, sheer gift. The late Malcolm Muggeridge wrote towards the end of his life that he believed that life at all times, and in all circumstances, was a precious gift. So if someone tries to end his or her life before its time, even when that person is in the terminal stages of an illness, is that always to be seen as an act of ingratitude, a spurning of the creator's precious gift of life? It can be argued that the Christian Church already allows considerations of the quality of life to be taken into account. For if a person refuses burdensome treatment, or if he takes a drug for the control of pain that has the side-effect of shortening his life somewhat, implicit in this is the idea that it is not simply life as such which is valuable, but that the quality of life can also be taken into account. Ten days of pain-free life is better than two weeks' life full of pain and discomfort. So a person might say that her quality of life at the end is so poor that she wants to end her life now. In that case, she argues, it is not an expression of ingratitude. She remains deeply grateful for her life, for a life which has had a certain quality about it, but her life now does not have enough quality about it to make it worth prolonging.

Life is a gift, a precious gift. If it is argued that the point of having a gift is that it is handed over to us to do what we like with it, this is simply not true. For the gift might be precious in itself. When Winston Churchill was painted by Graham Sutherland, he so hated the resulting portrait that he had it destroyed. Perhaps he said that it had been given to him, it was his, he was entitled to do what he wanted with it. But suppose he were to have taken the same attitude to one of his ancestral portraits, a Rembrandt or a Titian? Would we not say that those paintings have value in themselves which deserves to be respected? No one is entitled simply to do what they want with such an item, even if they lay claim to ownership of it. When it comes to the gift of life, even if our experience of it is distressing, it still has a value in itself which is to be respected. So although I do not think that a person who takes the point of view outlined in the previous paragraph is thereby necessarily showing ingratitude – she might ask for a lethal dose and say a prayer of thanks for her life as she goes into unconsciousness – nevertheless, from an objective point of view, her life still has all the value of a gift of God.

Nor do I think such an act is necessarily an act of rebellion or hubris, as Barth suggested. However, to ask for assisted dying is to reach the point where you judge your life has no more point, no more worth or significance, and that no good can come out of prolonging it. Your life is no longer a gift worth having. But the gift is still precious in itself, and as a Christian I do not think it is possible to say that it has reached a point where no good can come out of it. For that reason, I do not think that assisted dying is something that Christians should seek for themselves.

A society which values all its members

I concluded the preceding section by saying that I did not think that a Christian should seek assistance in dying for him- or herself. But clearly someone who does not share the Christian faith, or its values, in this area is in a different position. Such people are desperately calling out for assistance in dying. They believe that their life not only has no more pleasure in it, only pain, but has no more point or purpose. For them there is no God who might give them a different evaluation of their life at this stage. Friends and relatives try to assure them that they are still hugely valued and will be cared for, but they insist that they would rather be gone from this life as quickly as possible. It is difficult to see why their request should be refused. However, that is not the same as saying that such a situation should be allowed for in legislation. Legislation to allow for it raises all the questions discussed in the first part of this chapter.

When those points were discussed, it was concluded that, in the state of Oregon at least, the worst fears of those who oppose such legislation were unfounded. There was no pressure on the old, frail and vulnerable to seek assistance in dying. There was no falling off of the value of palliative care. There was no slippage from assisted dying to assisted suicide or to non-voluntary euthanasia. However, that is not the end of the matter.

First, the legislation in Oregon has only been in place for a few years. It is totally unknown what might happen over a longer period of time. Second, Oregon is only one, relatively small state. It exists in a wider culture in a large country that is clearly watching what happens very carefully. It might be a very different situation if the whole of the United States allowed assisted dying.

I am inclined to think that over a longer time period, of decades at least, and if the kind of legislation that exists in Oregon was put in place all over the United States and Europe, there would be slippage. I say this not on the basis that human beings are wicked and unless we are stopped we will do wicked things to one another. That may be true, but it is not my argument here. My argument here is based first of all on the fact that the case for helping people who are not terminally ill to commit suicide is just as appealing, if not more so, than the case for helping people who are actually dying. When I think of the young man totally paralysed as a result of a rugby accident, who had nothing to look forward to except helplessness for 50 or more years, or a person whose life has been ruined by repeated periods of deep depression or recurring schizophrenia, it is difficult not to be moved. After all, someone who is dying may have only a few weeks to stick it out. A paraplegic who can do nothing for himself and who can hardly communicate might have a lifetime to endure with nothing that gives him satisfaction and nothing to look forward to.

What has brought about the great legislative changes in our society over the last 50 years has been an intellectual climate that might fairly be described as liberal-progressive. This has at its heart a sense of compassion and a respect for the individual choices that people make in their lives. Many of the changes brought about in this climate have been much needed and are to be warmly welcomed. But we cannot assume that every change in such a culture will be for its good. It seems to me highly likely that in such a culture, the issue of allowing assisted suicide to people in the kinds of situation referred to above will gather momentum. There are of course already voices which advocate it, including the people who run the Dignitas clinic in Switzerland. The logic of the liberal, compassionate mind is obvious. If we allow assistance for people who are dying, why should we not give help in committing suicide to people whose predicament is sometimes more appalling than that of those who are dying? It is true that some of these people can, and sadly do, commit suicide without any help from others. But some, such as paraplegics, could not do so without help, and others, say those suffering from recurring, very deep depression, might understandably feel that death by a lethal dose prescribed by a doctor might be more certain and a lot less gruesome than cutting their wrists in a bath or taking an overdose of aspirin.

The situation in Belgium, where voluntary euthanasia has been allowed since 2002, is interesting. Anyone over 18 and in great distress can apply to be put to death by a doctor. They do not have to be dying. Strict safeguards seem to be in place, and on average about 31 people a month take this route.

On what grounds might one oppose this development? Most people would personally refuse a friend's request for help in killing themselves. This is not just because it is illegal at the moment, but because to accede to it would be saying, in effect, that you agree that your friend's life has no continuing worth. Most people would refuse to help a friend kill him- or herself and would look instead for ways of helping that friend find life more bearable. If this is how we respond as individuals, then this is the response also that a civilized society should make – and which ours does now. By forbidding people to help others commit suicide we are, as a society, implicitly making the point that everyone in our society, in whatever state of mental or physical distress, is of value. Everyone, without exception. If it is argued that this is unfair, because people should be allowed to make up their own minds as to whether or not their lives have any value, and we should not allow one moral norm to override individual freedom in this sphere, then this points to another very interesting fact. It means that our society is at the moment built on Christian foundations. Not everyone shares the Christian faith, but the fact that everyone, however disabled, is regarded as of worth in this way, is a Christian value, which in our society is widely shared by people who have a different or no faith.[23]

It could be argued that there are two different issues here, and that they need to be considered separately. One is whether we should legislate to let people seek assistance in dying. The other is whether we should legislate to let people who are not dying seek help in committing suicide. We could legislate for the first without the second necessarily following on. In a similar way, as I have argued in the first chapter of this book, we have legislated to allow research on the very early embryo. The question of research on the foetus in the womb is an entirely separate question, and one which, so I argued, is not likely to arise as a consequence of allowing research on the early embryo. But the link in that case between the two areas of research is rather different from the link between assisted dying and assisted suicide. This latter link is a natural expression of what I have termed the liberal-compassionate mind. If you are moved by the distress of someone dying, you are likely to be even more moved by the thought of someone 'locked in' on themselves for a lifetime. Although there are compassionate considerations to do with the health of unborn children behind research on the early embryo, and the same consideration might be brought to bear to drive research on the foetus in the womb (or an artificial womb) the instinctive reaction to this is very different. The foetus has a developing nervous system and at a certain point can feel pain. The foetus is a human individual, and we do not believe that humans should be treated instrumentally, that is, as means to some other end.

So there is a real fear that legislating to allow for assistance in dying would, over the course of time, in a cultural climate dominated by liberal progressivism, lead on to legislation to allow people in distress to seek help in committing suicide – or, as in Belgium, to allow them to apply for euthanasia administered by a doctor. For that reason it is better to draw a clear line, now, and oppose legislation that would allow for assistance in dying, even though this will undoubtedly add to some people's distress. On the positive side, refusing to allow for such a law makes an implicit statement to everyone who is dying that their life, from the standpoint of society as a whole, remains of value, whatever they personally may feel about it.

Biographical and biological life

In recent years it has been usual to make a distinction between biographical life and biological life. Biographical life does not of course mean life without a body, or imply that we are only mind loosely related to our bodies. The Christian view of the human person is that we are psychosomatic unities, an integral union of body, mind and spirit. Or, to put it another way, we are embodied selves. Biological life, however, focuses simply on bodily life. If a person has suffered a severe brain injury, we might say that there is biological life but no biographical life.

This distinction has become important because a number of distinguished Roman Catholic theologians have taken the view that when we are considering the human person we cannot simply think in terms of biographical life. We have to take biological life as a definitive indicator of the presence of a human person. This debate comes to the fore particularly over the issue of those diagnosed as being in a permanent vegetative state. This is a mysterious condition, not fully understood yet. There is biological life, for the person goes on breathing and living. But the cerebral cortex is destroyed and there is no brain activity. The 'person' lies there with eyes wide open, totally unresponsive to anything, in a state of 'chronic wakefulness without awareness'. Such a state needs to be distinguished from two other states. One is brain death. If a person is on a life-support machine and his heart and lungs are kept going, as a result he may look alive. But in fact he may be shown, as a result of certain tests on the brain, to be dead – hence the phrase brain death. The result is that if the life-support machine is switched off, the body will no longer function. The other condition is a deep coma. In a deep coma there is still some brain activity. Brain death has not occurred, and nor is it a permanent vegetative state, when there is no brain activity.

There have been one or two startling cases of a person having been diagnosed as being in a PVS and then having regained some conscious existence. On examination, however, it has been revealed that the original diagnosis was flawed. For example, Mrs Coons, an 86-year-old American patient, was prematurely diagnosed as being in a PVS after only four and a half months of unconsciousness. She later regained a degree of conscious existence. But she had not been examined by a neurologist, and her gerontologist considered that her condition might be attrib utable to other causes than PVS. His request for further tests to eliminate other factors was opposed by the patient's relatives. When proper time is allowed and the relevant specialists are consulted, there seems no reason to think that an accurate diagnosis cannot be made. The Medical Ethics Committee of the British Medical Association (BMA) in their consultative paper of September 1992 recommended that, however early a physician thinks that a diagnosis of PVS is called for, 12 months should elapse before the state is indicated. This is a conservative judgement, in order to give the maximum chance of eliminating error. The committee further strongly recommended that in the very early stages every effort should be made to provide rehabilitative measures and exclude all other possible factors which might impair cognition.

Withdrawal of treatment: the Tony Bland case

In 1989 Tony Bland, then aged 17, was seriously injured in the Hillsborough football disaster, suffering severe brain damage. Medical opinion over the next three years was unanimous in diagnosing his condition as a permanent (then called persistent) vegetative state. With the support of Mr Bland's family and doctors, a legal ruling was sought that all life-sustaining treatment might be stopped and he be allowed to die. The trial judge granted the declaration sought, a decision upheld first by the Court of Appeal and then the House of Lords. The case raises the most fundamental issues about what it is to be a human person; in particular, in relation to the present discussion, it raises the question whether it was biological life, which Mr Bland clearly had, or biographical life, which he did not have, that defined him.

The House of Lords' decision was made on the basis of what would in the judgement of the doctors concerned, with the sanction of the court, be in Mr Bland's best interests, taking into account the quality of his life. The doctors had concluded that his best interests lay in not artificially prolonging his life. Lord Justice Hoffmann argued that if Mr Bland had been able to choose, he would have chosen to put an end to the humiliation of his being and the distress of his family. It would show greater respect to allow him to die than to keep him grotesquely alive.

The emphasis upon quality of life was a relevant consideration here, as it is in some other circumstances. However, it is important to note that this judgment took place in relation to the question of not prolonging life by artificial feeding and antibiotic drugs. Discussion about the quality of life does not have the same overriding character in relation to a person who is living without such medical treatment, for example, someone who is simply old or senile.

Furthermore, the court rather glossed over the difference between normal and exceptional forms of medical treatment, or between what is proportionate and disproportionate in the way of medical care. But this is a relevant question. For we are under an obligation to care for people who are dying, even if we are not under an obligation to treat them. The question of whether life-sustaining artificial feeding is a form of normal care or a medical treatment is therefore a relevant question. The BMA's Euthanasia Report considered that 'Feeding/gastrostomy tubes for nutrition and hydration are medical treatments and are warranted only when they make possible a decent life in which the patient can reasonably be thought to have a continued interest.'

In 1991 the Institute of Medical Ethics published its majority view that 'it can be morally justified to withdraw artificial nutrition and hydration from patients in persistent vegetative state'. This was supported by the BMA's 1988 report. The BMA's Medical Ethics Committee in its consultative paper of September 1992 concluded that 'in previous cases where the clinician judges there can be no realistic chance of improvement and two other doctors independently concur with that view, it would be reasonable to remove all forms of invasive treatment, including nutrition and hydration'.

This seems to me sound; indeed in its consultation paper the Medical Ethics Committee of the BMA drew on Roman Catholic and Anglican advice in reaching its own recommendation.

In most cases, 'normal care due to the sick person' includes the giving of food and liquid even if these have to be administered artificially. But when a permanent vegetative state has been diagnosed, this is not so. When a middle-aged person has major heart surgery, this may be both painful and expensive. But there is a due proportion between the means used and the end that is hoped for. That person has every chance of recovering and leading a reasonable life. When a PVS has been diagnosed, the condition is irrecoverable. We have in effect a living carcass. Continuing to administer antibiotics and food and liquid by tube are medical means that are disproportionate to the end. For there is no good to be achieved.

When a PVS has been identified there is a further question. Is it any longer meaningful to talk of the presence of a person? A person is someone who can respond, act and communicate. But in a PVS all higher functions of the brain have ceased to operate. The body can make some instinctive responses but cannot feed, suffer or know. This raises some of the most difficult and complex questions of philosophy about the relationship between the brain and a person. There is scope here for continuing medical work in order to make the criteria for identifying a PVS as certain as possible. Nevertheless it is possible to have confidence in the judgement of doctors, and increasingly so with improved techniques, that a diagnosis of PVS can be reached with some certainty. In that situation we have a body-in-the-bed, to which respect is due. But the person is, in the words of the distinguished American ethicist Paul Ramsey, 'irretrievably inaccessible to human care'. The test of this is whether it makes no difference whether the death is, in Ramsey's words, by 'an intravenous bubble' or by withdrawal of useless ordinary means, such as food and liquid. If a person is in a deep, permanent coma or in a PVS so that she feels no suffering and is aware of no human presence; if, as far as she is concerned, it makes no difference whether she is hastened on her way by an act of commission or omission; if she is beyond all forms of care – then there is no longer a person to be reached. Our duty towards the dying is to accompany them on their way and not abandon them before their time. But if the person has effectively gone, that obligation no longer exists.

An opposite point of view to this, taken by some scholars, mainly though not exclusively Roman Catholic, is that where there is still a functioning body we must assume there is still a person. These scholars take a biological and exterior view of the person rather than a biographical or inner one. On the basis of the high Christian evaluation of the body, they argue that the body is intrinsic to being a person, not just a means to something else like consciousness. They argue that even the brain-damaged retain a radical human capacity in that they are turned towards the possibility of thinking and choosing and loving. But while we can certainly agree that there is no person without a body, it seems odd to say that the body constitutes the very reality of a person. Nor does it seem to make sense to say that when a person is badly brain-damaged, with no possibility of recovering the capacity to think and choose and love, he or she should still be accorded the absolute respect due to a human person. In this life there is no person without a body. But the body itself, when for example kept functioning on a life-support machine after brain death has been identified, or when there is a diagnosis of a PVS or when the brain has been so severely damaged that there is no possibility of mental life, is not a person. In such cases it would seem to evacuate the word person of its true significance, if it is used of the body alone. Leading Roman Catholic theologians, however, who emphasize the importance of biological life, have taken a more conservative view on issues like PVS, disagreeing with the judges about the legitimacy of withdrawing nutrition and hydration.[24]

The judges in the Tony Bland case, both in the Court of Appeal and the House of Lords, gave a mixture of reasons for their decision. One judge took the view that when someone has been diagnosed as in a PVS then in fact 'the spirit has fled'. That is a vivid image, suggesting that though biological life is evident there is no biographical life and therefore no longer a person there. I agree with that.

The Bland case also brought to the fore some of the issues that were mentioned at the beginning of this chapter: the difference between ordinary and extraordinary means of care, and the difference between acts of commission and acts of omission. Both issues have been subject to extensive discussion in recent years.

Tony Bland was kept alive by artificial nutrition and hydration. That is, he was given food and water through a system of tubes into his stomach. Lord Goff of Chieveley, quoted in one of the appeals over the Bland case, gives the following description of what this can involve:

Mr Bland cannot swallow, and so cannot be spoon fed without a high risk that food will be inhaled into the lungs. He is fed by means of a tube, threaded through the nose and down into the stomach, through which liquefied food is mechanically pumped. His bowels are evacuated by enema. His bladder is drained by catheter. He has been subject to repeated bouts of infection infecting his urinary tract and chest, which are treated by antibiotics. Drugs have also been administered to reduce salivation, to reduce muscle tone and severe sweating and to encourage gastric emptying. A tracheostomy tube has been inserted and removed. Urino-genitary problems have required surgical intervention.

A patient in this condition requires very skilled nursing and close medical attention if he is to survive . . . without skilled nursing and close medical attention a PVS patient will quickly succumb to infection.

I have no doubt in my mind that Tony Bland was receiving a highly invasive form of treatment; in other words he was kept alive by extraordinary rather than ordinary means of care. This is clearly a burdensome form of treatment which a person has a moral right to refuse. In the case of Mr Bland he could not of course make the decision himself. It was made for him by the court on the application of the doctors.

When the tubes were removed, Tony Bland was allowed to die. It was physically impossible for him to receive food and water by ordinary means. His mouth was kept moist and his life gradually faded away over a period of ten days. Such a situation is obviously distressing for all those involved, and therefore gives rise to the question as to whether it would not have been much more humane simply to give him a lethal dose when the tubes were withdrawn so that he could die painlessly and quickly, rather than in a long drawn-out, distressing death. He was not given such a lethal dose, and the court could not recommend that he should, because the law, based on traditional Christian medical ethics, makes an important moral distinction between acts of commission and acts of omission.

It is wrong deliberately to kill someone who is posing no threat. It is not wrong to let a disease take its natural course if medical intervention has been refused or would be useless. However, in the case of someone diagnosed as in a PVS we must ask whether that distinction still holds, and certainly some of the judges in the Bland case were unhappy about it.

As mentioned above, the American ethicist Paul Ramsey took a traditional view on most issues, including the distinction between what is intended and what is foreseen but unintended. He was opposed to euthanasia, believing that it is our duty to care for the dying and communicate to them the fact that they are not alone. There can be no reason, as he put it, 'to hasten them from the here and now in which they still claim a faithful presence from us'. To assist the process of dying would be a sort of abandonment. However, he also argued that there are certain conditions where the distinction between acts of commission and omission no longer holds good, and that is when a person is 'irretrievably inaccessible to human care'. As mentioned, this is when it makes no difference to a person whether he dies by a lethal injection or by withdrawal of artificial hydration and nutrition. This is a situation which includes PVS patients but it might also include those who are severely brain-damaged but still showing signs of brain activity. This seems to me one of those boundary situations where the usual moral norms do not apply, and for which Parliament or the courts could make provision – if they did not judge that this might lead to a slippery slope in which lethal doses could be given in cases other than those in which the person was irretrievably inaccessible to human care.

Non-voluntary euthanasia

Non-voluntary euthanasia takes place when a person is given a lethal dose on the basis of a decision made on her behalf because that person is not in a position to make such a decision herself. This has sometimes occurred in the Netherlands with neonates, that is, very young babies, who are so disabled that they are judged to have no chance of a life with any quality to it at all. Instead of simply being allowed to die, they have been killed. Non-voluntary euthanasia could also occur in theory if, say, someone who had been in a deep coma for years but where there was still brain activity of some sort (in other words a different situation from a PVS) and was judged highly unlikely ever to come out of it, was given a lethal dose, at the request of the family and doctors, and with the permission of the court. At the moment this is not allowed in law. Whether it should be depends on whether Paul Ramsey's criteria are accepted as a legitimate basis for such decisions, and whether if they were it would create another slippery slope from situations where such criteria were fulfilled to one where they weren't. For example, suppose someone developed Alzheimer's and was no longer capable of making rational decisions for himself, so relatives asked that he be given a lethal dose. This would be an unacceptable extension for most people, including me.

Nigel Biggar, as I mentioned earlier, accepts the distinction between biographical and biological life and thinks that there is a prima facie moral case to administer non-voluntary euthanasia to people who have biological but not biographical life, perhaps as a result of a severe stroke. However, he adds the important qualification that this should only be allowed if it does not at the same time undermine society's sense of the preciousness of every human life.[25] Later in his book he makes the judgement that it would do just this, and he includes among the cases that could not therefore be allowed, the Tony Bland judgment and PVS patients more generally.[26] The reason is that in May 1995, not long after the 1993 Bland judgment, the Irish Supreme Court allowed the same withdrawal of artificial nutrition and hydration from someone who was not in a PVS and who 'retained some cognitive function'. Furthermore, four years later the BMA published influential guidelines on withdrawal of medical treatment not just for PVS but for patients with severe dementia or stroke.[27]

Biggar says that he would very much like to find some way of justifying the withdrawal of artificial nutrition and hydration from patients like Tony Bland, because he thinks that from a moral point of view alone, without taking into account the effects of legislating for them, such decisions could be justified. But he can find no way of making them legal without going down a slippery slope, as he thinks we have, with the BMA guidance.

It seems to me however that, rather unusually, Biggar is conflating too many disparate concerns. First, PVS is a very distinct condition. There is a body, but there is no person. 'The spirit has fled.' For this distinct condition the present legal position, which allows relatives and doctors to go to the courts to authorize withdrawal of artificial nutrition and hydration, seems entirely correct.

Second, where there is still some brain function, it seems to me that the criterion of Paul Ramsey about someone being 'irretrievably inaccessible to human care' is a good one to use, not just when deciding whether a person should be allowed to die, or deliberately hastened on his or her way, but when deciding whether that person should be kept alive by medical means at all. In short, where there is biological life but no biographical life, and the person has not left an advance directive, it is legitimate for family and doctors to try to make a judgement about what he or she would have wanted, and if there is uncertainty, to apply to a court for a decision.

But is this a slippery slope – one which in fact we are already on?

Earlier in this chapter I suggested that there is a slippery slope (which I designated slope one) from allowing assisted dying to allowing assisted suicide, because our society, being governed by an intellectual climate of liberal progressivism, cannot help being moved by the pleas of people who find life unbearable, whether or not they are dying. I argued that we should avoid getting on to this slope in the first place by resisting calls to legalize assisted dying.

The second type of slippery slope, from assisted dying or voluntary euthanasia to non-voluntary euthanasia, is according to Biggar already a reality. Much of the argument about this point resolves around how the evidence from the Netherlands is assessed. But even leaving aside that difficulty, there are further important factors to take into account when considering the possibility of this slippery slope. First, studies done on the situation in Australia, where euthanasia is illegal, seem to show that there are more instances of non-voluntary euthanasia than in the Netherlands where euthanasia is legal. Furthermore, there is no evidence available about the number of cases of non-voluntary euthanasia in the Netherlands before voluntary euthanasia was legalized. In short, the fact that there are cases of non-voluntary euthanasia now may simply reflect what was part of the culture anyway, without in any way being attributable to the fact that voluntary euthanasia is allowed. Emily Jackson makes the further point that all rule making involves grey areas, and therefore the possibility of a slippery slope.

It will have emerged from this discussion that these questions are not as clear-cut as some would like. People are keen to simplify the contrast between those who think there is a totally moral prohibition against all forms of euthanasia, and those who think that people have a right to decide when to die. But the issue is much more complex and nuanced than that, and the arguments for and against the various positions are much more finely balanced. On balance I think that it is in the best interest of our society that the law remains as it is, but I am aware that there are people in very distressing personal circumstances which will continue to make us question the legal situation.

One of the reasons the debate will go on is because of the consultation paper put out by the Director of Public Prosecutions in September 2009 about the circumstances in which a person should be brought to trial for assisting someone's suicide. This sets out a range of reasons which would count in favour of bringing such a person to trial and a further range which would count against doing so. These questions represent the current policy, but they are to be reviewed in the light of public consultation.[28] This policy, so long as it remained in force, would mean that assisting someone to kill him or herself would still be illegal, but under certain circumstances the person assisting would not be prosecuted. For example, if the man or woman who wanted to die was of sound mind and had repeatedly expressed a wish to die, while the person helping had no vested interest in the death, but only compassion for their companion's suffering, that person would not be prosecuted.

It remains to be seen whether or not such a policy will meet the objectives of those campaigning for a change in the law, or whether the new DPP guidelines will in fact be a Trojan horse allowing another bill to be brought to Parliament.

Over the last three decades the life sciences and medical technology have raised some of the most intellectually challenging questions of our time. In particular we have been forced to think again about the origin and the end of personal life and indeed what it is to be a human person made in the image of God. This book has been written in the conviction that science is a gift of God and that we have been given the responsibility to use its methods and applications for human well-being. At the same time the continually developing Christian tradition of ethical thinking has some crucial insights to contribute to the debate, though sometimes of a more nuanced kind than would give comfort to either the defenders or the opponents of traditional positions.

Notes

Preface

1 See Emily Jackson, *Medical Law: Text, Cases, and Materials*, 2nd edn (Oxford: OUP, 2009), ch. 15.

1 The beginning of life

1 Robert Winston, *A Child Against All Odds* (London: Bantam, 2006).
2 See G. R. Dunstan, *The Artifice of Ethics* (London: SCM Press, 1974), ch. 4, 'Born to Rule'.
3 For a fuller discussion of developments in recent years see Ruth Deech and Anna Smajdor, *From IVF to Immortality* (Oxford: OUP, 2007). Ruth Deech is a former chair of the HFEA.
4 St Augustine, *Quaestiones in Heptateuchum*, I, II n. 80.
5 For an extended version of this argument see my article 'Delivering Public Policy: The status of the embryo and tissue typing' in *Studies in Christian Ethics*, 18.1, 2005. Also my 'The moral status of the early embryo' in T. W. Bartel, ed., *Comparative Theology: Essays for Keith Ward* (London: SPCK, 2003). This is based on a reading of the tradition by the late Professor Gordon Dunstan in 'The Human Embryo in the Western Moral Tradition' in G. R. Dunstan and Mary Seller, eds, *The Status of the Human Embryo: Perspectives from Moral Tradition* (London: King Edward's Hospital Fund, 1988), pp. 39ff. For an alternative view see David Jones, *The Soul of the Embryo* (London: Continuum, 2004).
6 There were a number of reasons for the 1869 decision. One was a fear of falling populations in France and Italy. Another was a growing abhorrence of abortion. Whether by design or accident, the stress on fertilization, rather than implantation, as a key moment in conception, brought Catholic teaching

into line with medical thinking at that point, which stressed the continuity of development. What was not known at that time was the very high percentage of fertilized eggs that were lost anyway in nature. It was assumed that most fertilized eggs implanted. This is very far from being the case. Another question concerns the meaning of the word conception both in relation to this debate and in the doctrine of the immaculate conception of Mary, which had been promulgated 15 years earlier in 1854. Norman Ford, for example, has argued that it covered both what we understand as fertilization and implantation.

7 Mary Warnock later came to think that 'respect' was not a very good word and 'non-frivolity' might better capture what she wanted to say. In other words, there always have to be serious reasons for what is done. However, I think that the word respect, as long as it is not taken to mean absolute respect, is still the most adequate word.

8 HFEA Code of Practice, 8th edn, 2009, 15.13.

9 See Church of England Board for Social Responsibility, *Personal Origins*, 2nd edn (London: Church House Publishing, 1996).

10 Peter Byrne, 'The animation tradition in the light of Christian philosophy', in G. R. Dunstan and Mary J. Seller, eds, *The Status of the Human Embryo* (Oxford: OUP, 1988), p. 99.

11 Robert Song, 'To Be Willing to Kill What for All One Knows is a Person is To Be Willing to Kill a Person', in Ronald Cole Turner and Brent Waters, eds, *God and the Embryo: Religious Perspectives on the Debate over Stem Cells and Cloning* (Washington, DC: Georgetown University Press, 2003), pp. 98–107. The title of Song's article is a quotation from the Roman Catholic theologian Germain Grisez.

12 Mary Warnock, in a personal communication to the author.

13 Anthony Kenny, review of *The Soul of the Embryo* in *The Times Literary Supplement*, 25 March 2005.

14 In Chapter 3 I consider the situation of those who are described as being in a permanent vegetative state, when there appears to be no consciousness of any kind.
15 John Habgood, *Being a Person* (London: Hodder and Stoughton, 1998), p. 147.
16 Keith Ward, *Religion and Human Nature* (Oxford: OUP, 1998), p. 147.
17 Ward, *Religion and Human Nature*, p. 158.
18 'That Nature is a Heraclitean Fire and of the Comfort of the Resurrection', *The Poems of Gerard Manley Hopkins*, ed. W. H. Gardner and N. H. MacKenzie (Oxford: OUP, 1970).
19 An argument advanced by Onora O'Neill, 'Stem Cells: Ethics, Legislation and Regulation', *Comptes Rendus Biologies*, 326.7 (2003), pp. 673–6.
20 As argued for example by Jonathan Glover, *The Guardian*, 6 May 2006.
21 Winston, *A Child Against All Odds*, p. 253.
22 Winston, *A Child Against All Odds*, p. 255.
23 Recommendation 17, paras 41–3, *Government response to the Report from the Joint Committee on the Human Tissue and Embryos (Draft) Bill* (October 2007).
24 A working party of leading Christian moral theologians set up by Pope John XXIII recommended that the Church should drop its ban on the use of artificial means of contraception in all circumstances. Their advice was rejected by Pope Paul VI in *Humanae vitae*. Behind the ban lies, I believe, a false understanding of what is the natural law given us by God. Natural law is not just nature left to its own processes, but, as argued earlier, humans using their God-given minds (which is what is natural for us) to interrelate with the processes of nature for human well-being. In the Anglican Communion successive Lambeth Conferences wrestled with this issue in the 1920s and 1930s and came to support the responsible use of contraception. See Richard

Harries, 'World Population and Birth Control', *Questioning Belief* (London: SPCK, 1995), ch. 11.

25 The Roman Catholic Church is opposed to in vitro fertilization not only because it results in some of the fertilized eggs being destroyed but because those who undertake this treatment 'dissociate the sexual act from the procreative act'. See the Roman Catholic Catechism, para 2377.

26 Winston, *A Child Against All Odds*, p. 183.

27 Dostoevsky brings this out in a classic passage in *The Brothers Karamazov*, where the Grand Inquisitor accuses Christ of treating human beings as free when they cannot cope with freedom and says 'We have had to correct your great work.'

28 The original purposes of research also included improving methods of contraception.

29 Dunstan and Seller, eds, *The Status of the Human Embryo: Perspectives from Moral Tradition*.

30 *Stem Cell Research: Report from the Select Committee*, Stationery Office, 2002.

2 Abortion

1 Emily Jackson, *Medical Law: Text, Cases, and Materials*, 2nd edn (Oxford: OUP, 2009) ch. 13.

2 The age beyond which it was illegal to have an abortion in category (a) was lowered from 28 to 24 weeks in 1990 because, as a result of improved medical and scientific techniques, babies born after 24 weeks are now viable.

3 According to Home Office figures of the time, between 30 and 50 women a year were dying from botched abortions, either criminally performed or self-induced. In addition there were an unknown number of suicides as a result of unwanted pregnancies. For the considerations which made David Steel, a Christian, want to move the bill and his attitude towards it now, see *Guardian* Society, 24 October 2007.

4 Critical care decisions raising ethical issues also arise in neonatal medicine. These are not considered in this book, but there is a full discussion in *Critical Care Decisions in Fetal and Neonatal Medicine: Ethical Issues* (London: Nuffield Council on Bioethics), 2006.

5 Polly Toynbee, *The Guardian*, 26 October 2007.

6 Margaret Olivia Little, 'Abortion, Intimacy and the Duty to Gestate', *Ethical Theory and Moral Practice* 2 (1999), pp. 295–312.

7 Jackson, *Medical Law*, p. 659.

8 Catharine A. MacKinnon, *Women's Lives, Men's Laws* (Harvard UP, 2005) p. 140.

9 Adrienne Rich, *Of Woman Born: Motherhood as Experience and Institution* (New York: Norton, 1976) p. 64.

10 Ronald Dworkin, *Life's Dominion* (London: HarperCollins, 1993), p. 16.

11 Ronald Dworkin, *Taking Rights Seriously* (London: Duckworth, 1978).

12 Christopher Miles Coope, *Worth and Welfare in the Controversy over Abortion* (Houndmills: Palgrave Macmillan, 2006).

13 Coope, *Worth and Welfare in the Controversy over Abortion*, p. 333.

14 A weighty discussion of this is *The Ethics of Research Involving Animals* (London: Nuffield Council on Bioethics, 2005). It supports research under carefully controlled conditions with the important qualification that every effort is made to implement the three R's: Refine, Reduce and Replace. Refine the experiments so that discomfort to animals is lessened, reduce the number needed, and replace animal experiments by other means.

15 The position of the Church of England can best be seen in *Abortion: An Ethical Discussion* (Church Information Office, 1965) and *Abortion and the Church: What are the issues?* (London: Church House Publishing, 1993).

3 The end of life

1 The Church of England has, I believe, a solid track record in producing work in this area. *On Dying Well,* the report of a very distinguished working party containing philosophers, theologians, lawyers and palliative care specialists, was first published in 1975 and stood the test of time remarkably well. A revised edition with new material was published in 2000 by Church House Publishing. For those who wish to enter into the debate from the standpoint of traditional Christian moral theology, the best book is Nigel Biggar, *Aiming to Kill: The Ethics of Suicide and Euthanasia* (London: Darton, Longman & Todd, 2004). All the references to the best and most up-to-date academic discussion are in its text and it contains a comprehensive bibliography as well as advice for further reading on particular aspects of the debate. Paul Badham, *Is There a Christian Case for Assisted Dying? Voluntary Euthanasia Reassessed* (London: SPCK, 2009) sets out to offer a case for assisted dying from a specifically theological and biblical point of view.

2 For the wider ethical context and the law on this subject see Emily Jackson, *Medical Law: Text, Cases, and Materials,* 2nd edn (Oxford: OUP, 2009), ch. 17.

3 Anne Ridler, 'Too Much Skill', *New and Selected Poems* (London: Faber, 1988), p. 68. (Permission applied for.)

4 Private letter to the author.

5 In Belgium euthanasia is integrated into the palliative care system.

6 Biggar, *Aiming to Kill.*

7 Badham, *Is There a Christian Case for Assisted Dying?*

8 Biggar's book focuses on the evidence from the Netherlands; this evidence is differently assessed by Badham, who argues that there has been no slippage there. Because Biggar's book was written in 2004 he does not consider the Joffe bills, but neither does he assess the evidence from Oregon.

9 Full details of the Oregon figures can be found at <http://oregon.gov/DHS/ph/pas/index.shtml>.

10 Badham, *Is There a Christian Case for Assisted Dying?* p. 112.

11 Evidence to an All Party Parliamentary Group by Ann Jackson, quoted in Badham, *Is There a Christian Case for Assisted Dying?* p. 114.

12 Quoted in Badham, *Is There a Christian Case for Assisted Dying?* p. 115.

13 Polly Toynbee's view is coloured by what she describes as the very distressing death of her mother. Apparently at one point her mother cried out, 'Where is Dr Shipman when you need him?'

14 Polly Toynbee, *The Guardian*, 1 August 2009.

15 I have argued this in *The Re-enchantment of Morality* (London: SPCK, 2008).

16 They are not innocent in the sense that they are guiltless, but because they constitute no threat or harm.

17 Church of England Board of Social Responsibility, *On Dying Well: An Anglican Contribution to the Debate on Euthanasia*, revd edn (London: Church Information Office, 2000), p. 61.

18 Edwin Muir, 'One Foot in Eden', *Collected Poems* (London: Faber, 1984), p. 227. (Permission applied for.)

19 It probably had a more technical meaning at the time, referring to the time of trial that was predicted would come with the ushering in of the Messianic age.

20 Quoted in Badham, *Is There a Christian Case for Assisted Dying?* p. 60.

21 Pierre Teilhard de Chardin, *The Divine Milieu* (Eastbourne: Sussex Academic Press, 2004).

22 Jean-Dominique Bauby, *The Diving Bell and the Butterfly* (London: Fourth Estate, 1997), pp. 77–8. Quoted in Biggar, *Aiming to Kill*, p. 42.

23 I am not of course claiming that everyone, especially the disabled, is treated as of worth in practice in other spheres.

I am talking quite specifically about the law, its effects and its implications.

24 In the paper drawn up jointly by Roman Catholic and Anglican bishops on euthanasia and related issues, there was total unanimity on all points but a certain glossing over the question of PVS because of a concern that a difference might arise over this. Official Roman Catholic statements on PVS tend to take the view that because it is not certain whether or not an individual diagnosed as in a PVS is still to be afforded all the rights and respect due to a person, it is best to take the safer course morally and act on the assumption that they are such.

25 Biggar, *Aiming to Kill*, p. 114.

26 Biggar, *Aiming to Kill*, pp. 168–71.

27 *Withholding and Withdrawing Life-prolonging Treatments: Good Practice for Decision Making* (London: BMJ, 1999); *Withholding and Withdrawing Life-prolonging Medical Treatment: Guidance for Decision-making* (London: General Medical Council, 2002).

28 As a result of the public consultation, the guidelines were refined, and from March 2010 represent official policy.